Welcome to xtb Issue Nine

Way to Go

XTB stands for **eXplore The Bible**.

Read a bit of the Bible each day and...

• Discover the 'Big Picture' of the Bible with the help of your free book.

• Read about Jesus and His miracles in the Gospel of **John**.

• Find out more about King David in the book of **2 Samuel**.

Are you ready to explore the Bible? Fill in the bookmark...
...then turn over the page to start exploring with XTB!

T...............................

Sometimes I'm called

.... **(nickname)**

My birthday is

....

My age is

....

My favourite 'way to go' is
(by bike? skateboard? blades...?)

....

....

Table Talk FOR FAMILIES

Look out for **Table Talk** — a book to help children and adults explore the Bible together. It can be used by:

• Families
• One adult with one child
• Children's leaders with their groups
• Any other way you want to try

Table Talk uses the same Bible passages as XTB so that they can be used together if wanted. You can buy Table Talk from your local Christian bookshop—or call us on **0845 225 0880** to order a copy.

OLD TESTAMENT	NEW TESTAMENT
Genesis	Matthew
Exodus	Mark
Leviticus	Luke
Numbers	**John**
Deuteronomy	**Acts**
Joshua	**Romans**
Judges	1 Corinthians
Ruth	2 Corinthians
1 Samuel	Galatians
2 Samuel	Ephesians
1 Kings	Philippians
2 Kings	Colossians
1 Chronicles	1 Thessalonians
2 Chronicles	2 Thessalonians
Ezra	1 Timothy
Nehemiah	2 Timothy
Esther	Titus
Job	Philemon
Psalms	**Hebrews**
Proverbs	James
Ecclesiastes	**1 Peter**
Song of Solomon	2 Peter
Isaiah	1 John
Jeremiah	2 John
Lamentations	3 John
Ezekiel	Jude
Daniel	**Revelation**
Hosea	
Joel	
Amos	
Obadiah	
Jonah	
Micah	
Nahum	
Habakkuk	
Zephaniah	
Haggai	
Zechariah	
Malachi	

How to find your way around the Bible

**Look out for the READ sign.
It tells you what Bible bit to read.** ⇨

**READ
Genesis 1v1-3**

**So, if the notes say... READ Genesis 1v1-3
...this means chapter 1 and verses 1 to 3
...and this is how you find it.**

Use the **Contents** page in your Bible to find where Genesis begins

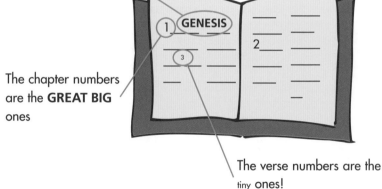

The chapter numbers are the **GREAT BIG** ones

The verse numbers are the tiny ones!

**Oops! Keep getting lost?
Cut out this bookmark and use it to keep your place.**

How to use xtb

1 Find a time and place when you can read the Bible each day.

2  Get your Bible, a pencil and your XTB notes.

3  Ask God to help you to understand what you read.

4  Read today's XTB page and Bible bit.

5  Pray about what you have read and learnt.

6  If you can, talk to an adult or a friend about what you've learnt.

YOUR FREE BOOKLET

This copy of XTB comes with a free booklet called **'Who will be King?'**.

This booklet will help us to see the 'Big Picture' of what the Bible's about, and to ask the very important question: 'Who will be your King?'.

We'll start at the very <u>beginning</u> of the Bible in the book of Genesis. **Are you ready to start? Then hurry on to Day 1.**

Don't worry if your free booklet is missing. Turn to the back page to find out how to get another copy.

THE BIG PICTURE

Welcome to **Way To Go** (Issue Nine of XTB). We're going to check out the 'Big Picture' of the Bible together.

The Bible is a H-U-G-E book! It has **1189** chapters!

If you read **three** chapters a day, it would take over a **year** to finish it!

If you've read **XTB** before, you'll know that we look at two or three Bible books in each issue. (This time, they'll be **John** and **2 Samuel**.)

But we're going to start by checking out the <u>whole</u> story of the Bible. Not by reading every chapter (phew!)—but by dipping in here and there to see the *'Big Picture'* of what the Bible's about. And we're going to use the free booklet **'Who will be King?'** to help us.

Let's start at the very beginning...

READ
Genesis 1v1

Fill in the gaps.

In the **b**_____,
God **c**_____ the heavens and the earth.

The Bible tells us that **God** made <u>everything</u>. He made our world, and everything in it. And He made <u>you</u>, too!

Now let's see what your free booklet says about this. Read the purple and green pages (pages 1–3) to find out.

As you read each new section of 'Who will be King?', you'll be learning a set of pictures. They sum up what the Bible is all about. Each time you learn a new picture, make a <u>copy</u> of it in the space on the next page.

Find out more on the next page.

IN THE BEGINNING......

xtb Genesis 1v1

You can keep your drawing very simple, like this:

God made the whole world and everything in it.
So draw a <u>circle</u> in the Day 1 box.

God makes people too, and gives us life.
Draw some <u>stick people</u> on the circle.

God is in charge of the world. He's the King.
Draw a <u>crown</u> above everything else.

Each time you read a new section of the booklet, come back to this page to add another picture.

Day 1

Day 5

Day 8

Day 4

Day 7

Day 10

The world God made is full of good things. What are some of your favourites?

1

2

3

PRAY

Thank God for the wonderful world He has made. Ask Him to help you to learn more about the *Big Picture* of the Bible in the next few days.

DAY 2 KING OF EVERYTHING

We're looking at the **Big Picture** of the Bible. Yesterday we started with the very first book in the Bible—**Genesis**. Today we're zooming to the other end—to **Revelation**.

READ
Revelation 4v11

There are some **tricky terms** in this verse. *Take the first letter of each picture to discover what they mean.*

'worthy to receive' means __ __ __ __ __ __ __

So God deserves to get something. What does He deserve? (v11)

g_____
h_____
p_____

This means we should treat God as the __ __ __ __ !

Why should we treat God as King?

Because He ' __ __ __ __ __ __ __ __ all things'.

This means that **God** made everything!

Read the green page again (page 3) in your **'Who will be King?'** booklet.

Fill in the gaps from the words at the top of page 3.

God is the L_____
K_____ of everything because
He m_____ everything.

PRAY

Do you believe that God made everything and is the loving King of everything? **If you do**, thank God for helping you to believe this. Ask Him to help you obey Him as your King. **If you're not sure**, ask God to help you learn more about Him as you read the Bible.

MISSING THE MARK

xtb Romans 3v23

Target Time: Make a small ball of play dough or sticky tack (or rolled up paper or a dry pea). Hold it high above the page, then drop it. What was your score?

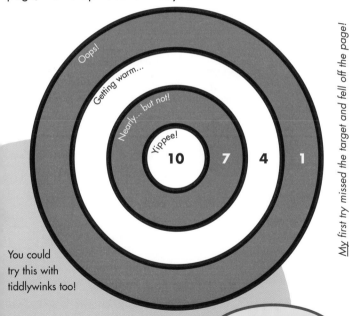

Oops!

Getting warm...

Nearly... but not!

Yippee!

10   7   4   1

My first try missed the target and fell off the page!

You could try this with tiddlywinks too!

What was that all about? *Read today's passage to find out.*

READ
Romans 3v23

What does this verse say we have **all** done? (v23)

S_____

Did you know?

Sin means 'missing the mark'. That's like aiming at a target, but <u>missing</u> the bullseye. It is **God** who sets the mark for us to aim at. He shows us in the Bible how to live a perfect life for Him. But we <u>all</u> miss the mark. We all sin.

Look again at the <u>last</u> sentence on the green page (page 3) of your booklet.

Who will be King?

What does it say?

> **The trouble is, we d_____ like doing what G_____ tells us to do...**

That's true for **all** of us. We do what <u>we</u> want, instead of what <u>God</u> wants—and we miss the mark!

PRAY Think of some ways that <u>you</u> have missed God's mark this week. (*eg: been cheeky, not been kind, told lies...*) Say sorry to God. Ask Him to help you change.

Yesterday we saw that **sin** means 'missing the mark'. *Crack the code to see what else* <u>sin</u> *means.*

— — — — — — — — — —

When people turn <u>against</u> their king, it's called a **rebellion**. <u>Sin</u> is when we turn against **God** as our King, and choose to be king of our own lives instead.

Next, check out another word from today's reading:

— — — — — — — — — —

To be 'righteous' means to be 'right with God'. It means that God will <u>accept</u> us—that nothing gets in the way between us and Him.

But there's a problem...

Who is **righteous** (acceptable to God) ?

 Everyone / Some / A few / No-one

READ
Romans 3v10-12

Crown Code

= B
= E
= G
= H
= I
= L
= N
= O
= R
= S
= T
= U

Wow! No-one is right with God! Not even one of us!

Turn to the page 5 (grey) of your free booklet to read what it says about that.

This picture shows what sin is like. We <u>don't</u> want God as our King (that's why the big crown is crossed out). We pretend that <u>we</u> are the king instead of <u>God</u> (so there's a small crown drawn over the person in the pic.)

Turn back to Day 1 and **copy** *this picture into the red box marked 'Day 4'.*

 PRAY

Sin isn't just about what we **do**. It's also how we **think**. When we think it's OK for <u>us</u> to choose how to live, rather than <u>God</u> saying how to live, then we're sinning. Say sorry to God for the times when you think like that.

"Mum said not to kick this indoors—but it won't matter."

"Oh no! Mum will be so cross!"

What do you think John's mum will do?

a) Say it doesn't matter, and give John some sweets.

b) Make John pay for a new vase with his pocket money.

John was **wrong** to play football indoors—and he knew it. He deserved to be **punished**. It wouldn't be right for his mum to say that it didn't **matter**.

Yesterday, we saw that everyone **sins**. We do what **we** want instead of what God wants. Sin **deserves** to be punished. It wouldn't be **right** for God to say that it doesn't matter.

Fit the yellow words into the puzzle.

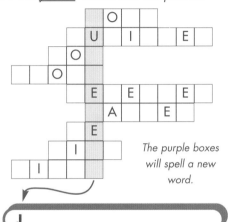

The purple boxes will spell a new word.

J

READ
Hebrews 9v27

God won't let us keep saying 'No' to Him. One day, everyone will be judged.

Find out more on page 7 (purple) of your booklet.

Who will be King?

Today's pic is like yesterday's, but with one big difference. Can you spot it?

God is the King of everything. *That's why the big crown is no longer crossed out.* God won't let people keep saying 'No' to Him. The punishment is that we are shut out of His kingdom for ever. *That's why the person is crossed out.*

Copy this picture into the box on Day 1.

PRAY

Say sorry to God for the wrong things you do that deserve His punishment.

DAY 6

 GOOD NEWS!

 Do you remember yesterday's cartoon about John breaking his mum's vase? John deserved to be punished. He had to pay for a new vase from his pocket money.

But what if someone offered to pay for the vase <u>instead</u> of John! How would John feel?

Today's Bible verse tells us that <u>Jesus</u> has done something a bit like that for us...

READ
1 Peter 3v18a

The 'a' means just read the <u>first</u> half of the verse.

Yesterday we saw that we <u>all</u> sin and deserve God's punishment. But what does today's verse say? (v18a)

Christ **d**_____ for **s**_____

Depending on which version of the Bible you are using, this verse may call Jesus **good**, or **innocent**, or **righteous** (which means 'right with God'.)

These are all ways of saying that Jesus <u>always</u> did what God wanted Him to do. He never said 'No' to God.

 That's odd! If Jesus never did anything wrong, why was He punished?

Great question! *Read the red page (page 9) of your booklet to find the answer.*

Fill in the gaps from the sentence at the top of page 9.

Jesus d_____ to take our

p_____

so that we could be

f_____.

PRAY Father God, thank you for sending Jesus to take our punishment so that we can be forgiven. Amen

AMAZING LOVE

Crack the Arrow Code.

⇦ ← ⬂ ▷ ⬇ ⬉ ◁ ⬈ ⬇ ▷ ▽ ▷

___ ___ ___ ___ ___ ___ ___ ___ ___ ___ ___ ___

◁ ← ⬂ ⬆ ⬇ ⬊ ← ◁ ▽ ▷

___ ___ ___ ___ ___ ___ ___ ___ ___ ___

The Bible tells us that **God** sent Jesus, His own Son, to die for us. **Why did God do that?** Read the red page of your booklet again (page 9) and see if you can spot the answer.

God sent Jesus because He is so **loving**. Circle love, loved and loving on the red page.

Wow! God's love is fantastic! Read about it in the most famous verse in the Bible.

READ
John 3v16

Arrow Code	
⬂	= D
⬇	= E
⬊	= F
⇦	= G
⬆	= I
⬈	= J
⬉	= N
←	= O
▽	= R
▷	= S
◁	= T
▽	= U

Fill in the gaps.

God L_____ the world so much
that He g_____ His only S_____,
so that everyone who
b_____ in Him may not die
but have e_____ life.

Wow! Everyone who trusts in Jesus can be forgiven and be with God for ever. What great news!

The picture shows that God is our loving King who sent Jesus to our world, to die for us. **Copy** this pic into the box on Day 1.

PRAY Thank God for loving you so much that He sent Jesus His Son to die for you.

DAY 8 KING OF THE WORLD

Wow One!

For the last two days we've thought about Jesus dying. He didn't deserve to die. He did nothing wrong. But He died to take the punishment **we** deserve, instead of us, so that we can be forgiven.

Cross out the X's to see Wow One...

XXJEXSXUSXXDXIDXN'TXXSTXAYXDEXADXX

Jesus <u>died</u> and took the punishment for us—but God brought Jesus back to <u>life</u> again! **Wow!** Read what **Peter**, one of Jesus' friends, said about Jesus...

READ
Acts 2v32

Fill in the gaps.

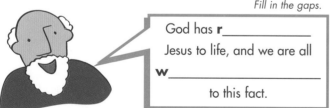

God has **r**_____
Jesus to life, and we are all
w_____
to this fact.

Peter was a **witness**. He had <u>seen</u> Jesus alive again!

Wow Two!

Jesus is <u>still</u> alive today. But He didn't stay here on our world. He went back to be with God, His Father.

READ
Acts 1v9-11

The two men in white were angels. What did they say Jesus will do? (v11)

He'll stay away / He'll come back

Wow Three!

God made Jesus the **King** of everything!
Read page 11 (blue) of your booklet to find out more.

Today's pic shows that **Jesus is King of the whole world**.
<u>Copy</u> it into the space on Day 1.
You can just put 'J' on the crown, if there isn't space to write 'Jesus'.

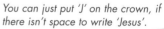

 PRAY Thank God for bringing Jesus back to life, and making Him the loving King of our world.

A CHOICE TO MAKE

 John 3v36

What is your free booklet called?

W _ _ _   _ _ _ _
_ _   K _ _ _ _ ?

This is a very important question. In fact, it's the most important question in the world!

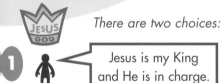

There are two choices:

1 Jesus is my King and He is in charge.

2 I'm in charge of my own life.

Read today's verse to see why this choice is so important...

READ
John 3v36

Take the first letter of each picture.

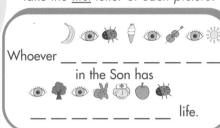

Whoever _ _ _ _ _ _ _ _ in the Son has _ _ _ _ _ _ _ _ life.

- '**Son**' means God's Son—Jesus.
- '**Eternal life**' means God being with us now, here on earth, and that we will live with Him for ever in heaven.

Whoever _ _ _ _ _ _ _ _ the Son will never share in that life.

- **BUT** if we keep saying 'No' to God and pretending to be our own king then God will shut us out of His kingdom for ever. We won't be with Him in heaven.

Wow! You can see why it's such an important choice!

Find out more on page 13 (yellow) in your booklet.

THINK + PRAY

This is such an important choice that we're going to think about it again tomorrow. While you are waiting, ask God to help you to understand and believe everything you have read today.

If you can't wait, it's OK to do tomorrow's page straight away!

As we saw yesterday, there are <u>two</u> ways to live:

<u>The first way</u> is to keep saying 'No' to God and pretending to be your own king. But if you do that, God will shut you out of His kingdom for ever.

<u>The second way</u> is to stop saying 'No' to God and ask God to forgive you. You can then start living with God's Son, Jesus, as your King.

Can you see how the two pictures match these two choices? In each pic, the <u>crown</u> shows who is king.

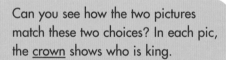

Copy this pic into the space on Day 1.

Counting the cost

It looks like a simple choice—and it is. But it needs thinking about carefully. There will be a <u>cost</u> for everyone who chooses to have Jesus as King.

*Cross out the **X**'s to see the cost.*

XWXROXXNXGXXSTXUXFFXX

- There will be some wrong things you have to stop doing.

XXFXXRIXXEXXNDXSXX

- Some of your friends may not like it when you change. They may laugh at you instead of being your friends.

XBXIBXLEXANXDXPRXAXYXERX

- You will need to make time to read your Bible, and to talk to God. You may need to stop something else (e.g. skipping a TV show) to make time.

READ **John 3v36** (again!)

Now read the page 15 of your booklet—***twice!***

THINK+PRAY

- ***If*** you already know that Jesus is King of your life, then <u>thank Jesus</u> for this. <u>Ask Him</u> to help you keep on living for Him every day.
- ***If*** you want to start living with Jesus as your King, then use the words at the bottom of page 15 to talk to God. Read the back cover of your booklet for some ideas of what to do next.
- ***If*** you're <u>not sure</u> if you want Jesus to be your King, ask an older Christian to talk to you about it. And ask God to help you understand and believe what they tell you.

If you have any questions, you can email at alison@thegoodbook.co.uk or write to at the address inside the front co

THE STORY SO FAR...

 xtb The Book of 2 Samuel

Welcome to the book of **2 Samuel**.

> **1 Samuel** and **2 Samuel** are really just <u>one</u> book. But it was such a **B-I-G** book, that it was split into two parts!

We're going to start by checking out the story so far from **1 Samuel**...

Chapter 1

Hannah was very unhappy because she had no children.

 GO

Hannah asked God to give her a son—and He did. Her son was called Samuel.

Chapters 2 – 7

Samuel grew up in God's temple. He loved and served God all his life.

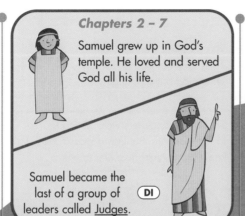

Samuel became the last of a group of leaders called <u>Judges</u>. **DI**

Chapter 8

When Samuel was an old man, the Israelites asked for a king to lead them.

ST

But the Israelites already had a king! <u>God</u> was their real King.

Chapters 9 – 12

God chose Saul to be the first king of Israel.

HE

Saul was very tall, very handsome, and a good soldier. He <u>looked</u> like a great king!

Chapters 13 – 15

Saul <u>looked</u> great—but he wasn't! He disobeyed God's rules.

RE

Saul turned away from God, so God took away the right of Saul's family to be kings.

Turn to the next page to find out more.

1 Samuel
17v45-50

Chapter 16

God chose a new king, instead of Saul. He would be king when Saul died.

AL

The new king was called David.

Chapter 16v7

David was a young shepherd when God chose him. He didn't <u>look</u> much like a king!

But God knew what David's heart was like. God knew David loved and trusted Him.

'Man looks at the outward appearance, but God looks at <u>the heart</u>.'
1 Samuel 16v7 **KI**

Chapter 17

The Israelites were at war. Their enemies had a HUGE champion called Goliath.

NG

Saul and his soldiers were all too scared to fight Goliath. But David wasn't. He knew God would help him to win...

READ
1 Samuel 17v45-50

You are coming against me with **sw**_____, and **sp**_____ and **J**_____, but I come against you in the name of the **LORD A**_____.

(v45)

David <u>trusted</u> God to help him win— and he was right!

You will find two letters hidden in each cartoon. Copy them (in order) into the space below to discover something important that David knew about God.

<u>G</u> __ __   __ __   __ __ __

__ __ __ __   __ __ __ __

PRAY

David knew a lot about God. He knew that God would rescue Him from Goliath, so that everyone would know that God is the Real King (v46). Ask God to help you to learn more about Him as you read 2 Samuel. Ask Him to help you trust Him as much as David did.

DAY 12 WAITING FOR GOD

God had chosen David to be king of Israel after Saul died. But Saul became very <u>jealous</u> of David—and kept trying to kill him!

David used to play the harp for Saul. But one day, Saul suddenly threw a spear at David! David had to dodge out the way.

Another time, even though David was married to Saul's daughter, Saul sent men to David's room to kill him. David escaped by climbing out of the window!

David had to run away from Saul's palace. But Saul kept chasing David...

One day, Saul took an army of 3000 men to search for David. At night, Saul slept on the ground in the middle of his army. There were thousands of soldiers around Saul, but even so David and one of his men (called Abishai) crept right up to where Saul was sleeping...

READ
1 Samuel 26v7-12

David and Abishai were right next to Saul. They could easily kill him! So why didn't they? (v10)

a) David was scared because Saul's soldiers were so close.

b) David knew that God would decide the right time for Saul to die.

c) David wanted Abishai to kill Saul later.

THINK SPOT 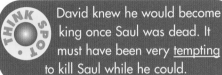 David knew he would become king once Saul was dead. It must have been very <u>tempting</u> to kill Saul while he could.

Copy all the <u>red</u> letters (in order) to see what David chose to do.

_ _ _ _ _ _ _ _

_ _ _ _

PRAY David knew he could trust God. He knew God would do the right thing at the right time. God's ways are <u>always</u> best. Ask God to help you to trust Him—even when that means waiting a while.

As we'll find out tomorrow, this was the last time that David saw Saul...

DAY 13 A MESSY START

2 Samuel starts with a man with torn clothes and dirt on his head! He had a message for David...

READ
2 Samuel 1v1-4

Who was dead? (v4)   **S**_____

and **J**_____

As we saw yesterday, Saul tried many times to <u>kill</u> David. How do you think David felt now that Saul was dead?
Circle your answer or add one of your own.

surprised   sad   relieved
happy   lonely

READ
2 Samuel 1v11-12

What did David and his men do? (v11)

_____ their clothes

Did you know?

Tearing your clothes was a sign that you were very sad or upset. People in Bible times did this when they heard terrible news.

Saul had tried to kill David many times. But David knew God had chosen Saul to be king. So he was upset that God's chosen king was dead.

A Fishy Story

The messenger said that <u>he</u> had killed Saul (which he probably didn't, since 1 Sam 31v4 says Saul killed himself). Maybe the messenger thought David would reward him for killing his enemy Saul. But he was wrong! *'How is it that you dared to kill the Lord's chosen king?'* asked David (v14)—and he had the messenger killed.

THINK+PRAY

This seems a sad, messy start to 2 Samuel, full of deaths and lies. But in the middle of the mess, notice that <u>God's plans</u> are working out. Yesterday we saw that David <u>waited</u> for God to decide when he would become king. Now that day was coming. David would be the new king, just as God had promised.
Thank God that His plans always work out, even though sad things happen to His people sometimes.

DAY 14 SAD SONG

How are you feeling right now? _Draw_ your answer here. ➡

If you're happy—great! But it's OK to be sad sometimes. David was really upset about the deaths of Saul and his son Jonathan.

Crack the code to see how David showed his sorrow.

___ ___ ___ ___ ___ ___ ___

READ
2 Samuel 1v17-18

A **lament** is a poem or song about your sadness. David wrote about his sadness at the deaths of Saul and Jonathan.

Read part of David's lament for yourself.

READ
2 Samuel 1v23-27

Face Code

 = A

 = E

 = L

 = M

 = N

= T

Fill in the gaps.
Saul and Jonathan were both brave soldiers.
They were swifter than **e**_____,
and stronger than **L**_____. (v23)
The women of Israel were to weep for **S**_____. (v24)
David grieved (was very upset) for **J**_____
because Jonathan was very **d**_____ to him. (v26)

Jonathan had been David's best friend. He had even protected David from his father, Saul!

THINK SPOT It's very sad when someone you love dies. God hates death too and the worst thing is that death can separate us from Him for ever. That's why God sent Jesus. Jesus can make death harmless for His followers.

PRAY If you are a Christian (a follower of Jesus) then even _death_ will never separate you from the love of your best friend, Jesus. Thank Him for this.

If you have time, check out **Romans 8v35-39** to see a l-o-n-g list of things that _can't_ separate you from Jesus' love!

KING AT LAST

xtb 2 Samuel 2v4a & 5v1-5

Now that Saul was dead, it was time for God's promise to David to come true. But it didn't happen all at once...

Take the first letter of each pic

1 King of _ _ _ _ _

After Saul's death, David went to live in the town of Hebron.

**READ
2 Samuel 2v4a**

The 'a' means just read the <u>first</u> part of the verse.

David was **a**_____
as king of **J**_____

'Anointed' means David had oil poured on his head to show he was king.

Israel was divided into <u>twelve</u> family groups called **tribes**. David was now king of the tribe of <u>Judah</u>. But Saul's son, Ishbosheth, became king of the rest of the Israelites. The two king's armies were at war for seven years. Finally, Ishbosheth was killed by David's men.
(*This is in 2 Samuel 2–4.*)

2 King of _ _ _ _ _ _ _

**READ
2 Samuel 5v1-5**

How old was David when he became king? (v4)   _____ years old

How long did David rule as king? (v4)   _____ years

In verse 2 we find that the Israelites had remembered something very important:

_ _ _ _ _ _ ' _ _ _ _ _ _ _ _

They knew that **God** had said David would be their king. (*God's promise is in 1 Samuel 16v12.*)

THINK+PRAY

God had first chosen David to be king when he was only a teenager. But it didn't happen straight away. Even after Saul had died, David only became king of <u>one</u> tribe (Judah). He had to wait another seven years to become king of Israel. But God **kept** His promise. David was now king!
God's words <u>always</u> come true. Think (or ask someone) about some promises of God that haven't happened yet. Ask God to help you wait and trust Him.

Yesterday, we saw that God's words always come true, but that we sometimes have to wait for Him to keep His promises.

Let's jump back in time, **800 years** before David was born, to a promise made to Abraham...

Don't worry about the long names.
Just have fun trying to say them!

Girgashites??

"I promise to give your family the lands of the Kenites, the Kenizites, the Kadmonites, the Hittites, the Perizzites, the Rephaites, the Amorites, the Canaanites, the Girgashites,

and the _ _ _ _ _ _ _ _ _ _ _ _ ." Genesis 15v18-21

800 years later, David was king over Abraham's family (the Israelites). The time had come for God to keep His promise...

READ
2 Samuel 5v6-10

What did the Jebusites say? (v6)

You will never get in here; even the

b_____ and the

_____ could keep you out!

But they were wrong! David and his men captured Jerusalem from the Jebusites (possibly by climbing up a water tunnel under the city).

How did David become so powerful? (v10)

Because the **L**_____ **G**_____
A_____ was with him.

Jerusalem became the royal city—where the king lived. David built a palace there, for him and his family to live in. (v11-16)

PRAY

Wow! God was <u>with</u> David. And He kept the promise He had made to Abraham 800 years earlier. God <u>always</u> keeps His promises. Neither 800 years nor strong enemies can stop Him! Thank God that nothing (and no-one!) can stop His words coming true.

Read round the spiral to see another promise God had made.

"I will use my servant David to rescue my people Israel from the Philistines." 2 Samuel 3v18

Let's see how God does it...

VICTORY ONE

READ
2 Samuel 5v17-21

Who did David ask before he attacked the Philistines? (v19)

[   ]

What did God tell David? (v19)
a) Yes, I will give you victory.
b) No, the Philistines will beat you.

Did David win the battle? (v20)

Yes / No

THINK SPOT
Before fighting the Philistines, David asked God what to do. That's a <u>top tip</u> for us, too. If you're not sure about something, **ask God** to show you what to do.

VICTORY TWO

READ
2 Samuel 5v22-25

What did God tell David this time? (v23)
a) Attack from here, and you will win.
b) Circle around behind them first.

What was David to listen for? (v24)
a) The sound of the wind in the trees.
b) The sound of marching in the trees.
c) The sound of monkeys in the trees.

Did David win this time? (v25)

Yes / No

THINK+PRAY

The Old T is great for showing us what God is like! On Day 15 we learnt that God's words always come true, but that we sometimes have to wait. On Day 16 we saw that nothing and no-one can stop God's plans. And today we've seen how God showed David what to do, so that His promise about the Philistines came true.
*God shows **us** what to do too!—in the Bible. Ask God to help you to trust Him and obey Him as David did.*

DAY 18 RESPECT!

God helped David and the Israelites capture Jerusalem. It was now the royal city. But there's something missing!

Follow the maze to see what it was.

T	V	O	F	O
N	E	C	T	K
A	N	E	H	R
	T	H	E	A

T _ _ _ _ _ _ _ _ _ _ _ _ _ _ _ _

Did you know?

The Ark of the Covenant (The Covenant Box)
The ark was a wooden box, covered in gold. Inside the ark were two stone tablets with the Ten Commandments written on them. The ark reminded the Israelites that **God was with them**.

God had given clear rules about moving the ark. It was to be covered by the priests, then carried on its poles (Numbers 4v15). And no-one was to <u>touch</u> the ark, or they would be killed! But read what happened...

READ
2 Samuel 6v3-7

How did they carry the ark? (v3)   On a **c**_____

Who touched the ark? (v6)   **U**_____

Uzzah broke God's rules, and he was killed.

THINK SPOT Does that seem too hard? If so, remember that the ark was a sign of our great, powerful God. He didn't want anyone to be killed. That's why His rule warned them <u>not</u> to touch the ark. But God must be treated with **respect**. His rules should never be ignored.

David was angry about Uzzah's death. And he was afraid of God. So he left the ark with someone else, rather than take it to Jerusalem. (v8-11)

PRAY In the past few days we've seen that God's words always come true. Today we've learnt that God is also powerful and dangerous. He's dangerous for those who don't listen to Him or obey Him. But (as we'll see tomorrow) He's fantastic if we listen and obey Him. Ask God to help you do that, especially when you don't want to.

If you've found today's page hard to understand or scary, talk to an older Christian about it.

xtb

2 Samuel
6v12-15

The story so far...

- King David captured Jerusalem and made it his royal city.
- He wanted to bring the ark there.
- But when Uzzah was killed for touching the ark, David was scared.
- David left the ark with a man called Obed–Edom. While it was there, God was very kind to Obed–Edom.

READ
2 Samuel 6v12-15

David realised that **Obed–Edom** was being **blessed** (given good things) because he was looking after the **ark**. So David went to bring the ark to **Jerusalem**. He made **sacrifices** (gifts) to God. Then everyone **shouted** and played **trumpets**, while David **danced** for God.

Fit the blue words into the puzzle.

		S	A	C					
			C	E					
				S	S				
	M	P							
			E	D	–	E	D		
		A	R						
			V	I					
S	H								
			U	S					

The yellow boxes will spell a new word.

C_____

David and the Israelites realised that having God with them wasn't just a <u>scary</u> thing. It was also a <u>brilliant</u> thing, worth ***celebrating!***

THINK SPOT

The ark reminded the Israelites that ***God was with them***. If <u>you</u> are a Christian (a follower of Jesus) then God is with **you** all the time. That's something to celebrate!

How will <u>you</u> celebrate that **God is with you**? You could...

**THINK
+
PRAY**

- tell God how happy you feel
- sing a song for Him
- play a happy tune on an instrument
- make a poster, showing how you feel about God
- or dance like David!

Choose one and do it now!

WINDOW WATCHING

Jon wants to help at church, but he's worried about what his mates will think. Today's story has something to say about that...

David was dancing in front of the ark as it came into Jerusalem. After the ark was put in a special tent, David made sacrifices (gifts) to God. Then he gave gifts of food to everyone in the crowd.

READ
2 Samuel 6v16-23

Michal was Saul's daughter and David's wife. Where did she watch David from? (v16)

A **w**_____

What did Michal think when she saw David dancing? (v16)

a) She was pleased and wanted to join in.
b) She was disgusted by his dancing.
c) She was bored and went to wash her hair.

Michal was disgusted that David wasn't acting like a king. She thought he was making a fool of himself in front of the people.

But what did David say? (v21) *Cross out the **X**'s.*

I will XCXELXEXBRXATXEX before the XLXORXDX

He wasn't dancing for the people. He was dancing for <u>God</u>!

THINK + PRAY

Are you like David? Or are you sometimes like Jon in our cartoon? Does worrying about what other people think ever stop you from praising or serving God? **Ask God** to help you to put Him first, and not worry about what other people think.

AMAZING GRACE

Find all the matching pairs. Which is the odd one out?

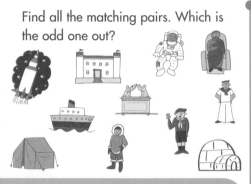

King David now lived in a <u>palace</u> built of beautiful cedar wood. But the ark of God didn't have a proper home! That bothered David. It didn't seem right...

READ
2 Samuel 7v1-3

Nathan was a *prophet* (one of God's messengers). What did he tell David? (v3)

a) Do whatever you have in mind
b) Don't do anything

But that night God gave Nathan a message for David. God <u>didn't</u> want David to build Him a temple. That would be someone else's job. Instead, God made amazing promises to David.

Crack the code to see God's promises.

⇧ ⇨ ⇩ ⇦ ↘ ↖ ◁ ▷ ◁
A C E G L P R S T
           ⇦ ◁ ⇩ ⇧ ◁

• I will make your name _ _ _ _ _ (v9)

    ↖ ↘ ⇧ ⇨ ⇩

• I will provide a _ _ _ _ _ for my people Israel to settle (v10)

    ◁ ⇩ ▷ ◁

• I will give you _ _ _ _ from your enemies (v11)

Read these promises for yourself:

READ
2 Samuel 7v8-11

What's this important Bible word? ⇦ ◁ ⇧ ⇨ ⇩
_ _ _ _ _

Did you know?

Grace is God's HUGE kindness to people who don't deserve it.

David had wanted to do something for God, but instead God promised to do great things for David! That's grace!

THINK + PRAY

Think of some of the great things God has done for you. (e.g. *answered your prayers, sent Jesus so that you can be His friend...*) Thank God for His huge kindness to you (His grace).

DAY 22 INDESTRUCTIBLE PROMISE

God had made some great promises to David—but He wasn't finished yet!

READ
2 Samuel 7v12-17

There are some tricky terms in those verses, so here's the **XTB Xplanation**.

After your death I will make your son the next _ _ _ _ (v12)

God promised that after David died, one of his sons would become king.

He will _ _ _ _ _ me a temple. (v13)

David had wanted to build a temple for God. Instead, his son would build it.

His _ _ _ _ _ _ _ _ will last for ever. (v13)

God promised that David's family would serve Him as kings for ever!

I will punish him when he does wrong, but my _ _ _ _ will never be taken away from him. (v14-15)   *Just like a human father, God would punish the king when he did wrong. But God would always love him.*

When we make promises they're often just for a short time...

> I promise to look after Tiddles while you're on holiday.

...or we don't keep them...

> You promised not to touch the cake before your party!

But God's promises aren't like that! God's promise to David lasted for ever...
—it wasn't broken when David <u>died</u> (v12)
—it wouldn't be broken when the king did <u>wrong</u> (sinned) (v14-15)
—this promise would last for <u>ever</u>! (v16)

PRAY

Thank God that <u>nothing</u> can stop His amazing promises coming true. Thank Him that we can trust Him completely.

DAY 23 CHRISTMAS IS COMING!

xtb   Luke 1v30-33

Can you add the missing words to these Christmas carols?

♪ **Once in royal** _____'s city

♪ **Away in a** _____

♪ **While** _____ watched

♪ **O little town of** _____

> Um... why are we suddenly singing carols???

Let's jump to the New Testament to find out. An angel has a message for a young woman called Mary...

READ
Luke 1v30-33

What was Mary's son called? (v31)

Which king does the angel talk about in verse 32?

How long would Jesus' kingdom last? (v33)

Wow! Look how <u>Jesus</u> matches God's promise to David: (*Use the missing words from the carols.*)

• Jesus came from **D**_____'s family. The angel said he would be a king from David's family line (v32).

• Jesus was born in **B**_____. (That's David's home town—that's why it's called 'royal David's city'.)

• Jesus was a king—but He wasn't born in a palace! Instead, He slept in a **m**_____ (an animal's food box), and the first people to see Him were a bunch of unimportant **s**_____.

• But the angel said that Jesus' kingdom would *last for ever!* (v33)

We'll find out more about King Jesus when we start reading the book of **John** *on Day 31.*

PRAY

God kept His promise to David by sending Jesus. **He** is the King who will rule for ever. Thank God for sending Jesus. Is He <u>your</u> King?

Answers: David's, manger, shepherds, Bethlehem.

DAY 24 DAVID'S PRAYER

We're going to Disneyland for a holiday.

You can have a pony for your birthday.

We'll buy you a new computer next week.

✔ *Tick the one you'd like best.*

How would you feel if this was promised to you?

God had made some <u>amazing</u> promises to David. We're going to listen in as David talks to God about how he feels...

READ
2 Samuel 7v18-22

What does David call God five times in these verses?

S_____ L_____

Did you know?

Sovereign means God is <u>in control</u> of everything. He is the ***Real King!***

What does David tell God? (v22)

How **g**_____ you are,
O Sovereign LORD! There is
n_____ like you.

Look at **verse 18**. Did David think he was someone great who deserved God's goodness? **Yes / No**

But God was **so** good to David! That's God's ***grace***. (Remember this word from Day 21?)

(Circle) the words that describe **you**.

important   well-known   perfect
powerful   rich   great

We're nothing special are we? But God has made amazing promises to us too! Keep reading the Bible to find out more.

(Circle) the words that describe what **God** is like. Add two more of your own.

sovereign   weak
uncaring   promise keeper
trustworthy   great   loving

PRAY   Now use these words in a thank you prayer to God.

DAY 25 VICTORY PARADE

2 Samuel 8v1-14

Chapter 8 lists David's victories over a bunch of enemies. *Find their names in the wordsearch. Some are backwards!*

PHILISTINES
MOABITES
ARAMEANS
EDOMITES
HADADEZER

G	O	D	P	R	O	M	I	S
E	D	H	A	D	A	D	E	Z	E	R
S	N	A	E	M	A	R	A	T	O	G
P	H	I	L	I	S	T	I	N	E	S
I	V	E	S	E	T	I	B	A	O	M
D	A	V	I	D	R	E	S	T	F	R
O	M	H	E	D	O	M	I	T	E	S
I	S	E	N	E	M	I	E	S

Why did David win so many battles? The answer is in verses 6 and 14. Look out for the <u>same</u> words in both verses...

READ
2 Samuel 8v6 + v14

Finish the sentence:

The LORD _____
_____

It was **God** who gave David all these victories! Copy the <u>leftover letters</u> from the wordsearch (in order) to find out why.

Some letters are already done to help you.

G __ __   P __ __ __ __ __ __ __ __

__ __ __ __   D __ __ __ __   R __ __

__ __ __ __ __ __ __   E __ __ __ __ __ __

This promise is in 2 Samuel 7v11

God is the **Promise–Maker** and **Promise–Keeper**. He is <u>always</u> faithful. (That means we can always trust God to do what He says.)

'The LORD is faithful to all His promises.' Psalm 145v13

Copy this verse from Psalm 145 on to some paper. Stick it on your bedroom wall or use it as a bookmark in your Bible. Say it aloud three times every day this week to learn it.

PRAY God is the Promise–Maker and Promise–Keeper. How does that make you feel? Talk to Him about it.

Ask an older Christian to show you some of God's promises to us.

DAY 26 WHAT KIND OF KING?

Yesterday we saw what Chapter Eight tells us about **God**. Now let's find out what it shows us about **David**...

READ
2 Samuel 8v7-11

What did David collect from his enemies?

- <u>G</u> __ __ __ shields (v7)
- <u>B</u> __ __ __ __ __ (v8)
- <u>S</u> __ __ __ __ __
  and <u>G</u> __ __ __ (v11)

*Shade in all the coins with **X**, **Y** or **Z** on them to see what David did with all this treasure.*

David **dedicated** the treasure—which means he gave it to God. It was probably kept to be used for God's temple.

READ
2 Samuel 8v15

What kind of king was David? (v15)

a) Just and fair.
b) Jolly and freckled.
c) Juggling and fat.

David was just and fair, doing what was <u>right</u> for his people.

This doesn't mean that David was **perfect**. There is only <u>one</u> perfect King in the world—**King Jesus!**

THINK + PRAY

David gave all the treasure to God. What can <u>you</u> give to God? You probably don't have much treasure! But can you think of a way that you can give God some of your *time*, or the *things you are good at*, or your *pocket money...?* Think carefully, then talk to God about your answers.

DAY 27 MEPHIBO-WHO?

 2 Samuel 9v1-13

David had been friends with Saul's son Jonathan. So David wanted to show kindness to anyone from Jonathan's family...

READ
2 Samuel 9v1-7

What was Jonathan's son called? (v6)
a) Mephistopheles
b) Mephibosheth
c) Metropolitan

Did you know?

Mephibosheth had been dropped by his nurse when he was five. As a result, he became crippled and couldn't walk. (2 Samuel 4v4)

What did David promise to do for Mephibosheth? (v7)

1. Show him **K**_____

2. Give him the **L**_____ that belonged to **S**_____

3. Let him eat at the royal **T**_____

Flag Code

▬	= D
▬	= E
●	= I
✕	= M
◥	= O
▭	= P
✚	= R
▪	= S

THINK SPOT

Mephibosheth was part of <u>Saul's</u> family. In those days kings would murder everyone from the previous king's family, in case they tried to become king themselves. But David <u>didn't</u> do that. *Crack the code to see why.*

David __ __ __ __ __ __ __ __ __ Jonathan.

David had promised not to harm any of Jonathan's family (1 Samuel 20v15). But David did <u>much</u> more than that. He also showed ***great kindness*** to Mephibosheth.

Who do <u>you</u> know who could do with some kindness? (*Someone in your class who gets left out? An old lady without many relatives?*)

THINK + PRAY

_____
What can you do for them?
_____
_____

Ask God to help you do it!

DAY 28 A PATTERN FOR US

 Romans 5v10

Only <u>two</u> of these patterns are exactly the same. Which two?

King David is like a <u>pattern</u> for us. He is God's chosen King, ruling over God's people (the Israelites) in the land God has promised to give them. What **David** does is sometimes a picture of what **God** does...

Yesterday we saw David showing <u>great kindness</u> to an enemy. (Mephibosheth came from Saul's family, so he would be seen as David's enemy.) Mephibosheth did nothing to deserve David's kindness. David was kind because of his **faithful love** for Jonathan. **God** is like that too!

READ
Romans 5v10

This verse is a bit tricky—so here's the **XTB Xplanation**... (*The answers are written backwards! If you get stuck, use a mirror to read them.*)

Once we were God's **enemies** _____.
But we have been brought **back** _____ to Him
because His **Son** _____ has died for us.

Wow! We were God's enemies because of our **sin** (doing what <u>we</u> want instead of what <u>God</u> wants). But God's Son, Jesus, died to take the punishment we deserve, so that we can be forgiven and be brought back to God.

To find out more, read the free booklet that came with this issue of XTB.

PRAY David's kindness to Mephibosheth was like a little picture of God's HUGE kindness to us. Thank God for His great kindness in sending Jesus.

Answer: The two identical patterns look like this.

DAY 29 A CLOSE SHAVE

King David is treating his people <u>fairly</u> (Day 26).
And showing <u>kindness</u> to Mephibosheth (Day 27).
But he's kind to people from other countries too...

READ
2 Samuel 10v1-2

King Nahash died, and his son Hanun became the next king of the Ammonites. What did David think? (v2)

I will show **k**_____ to
H_____, just as his
f_____ showed kindness to me.

*Hanun
father
kindness*

David sent some men with a kind message for Hanun—but Hanun didn't trust David...

READ
2 Samuel 10v3-5

What did Hanun do to David's men? (v4)

✔ *Tick the correct answers.*

- gave them all sweets ☐
- locked them in prison ☐
- shaved half their beards ☐
- called them rude names ☐
- cut their clothes, so their bottoms were showing! ☐
- made them eat slime ☐

This was a <u>terrible</u> insult. And by insulting **God's people**, they were insulting **God** too! *Tomorrow we'll see what David did about it...*

THINK + PRAY

Look back at what you wrote in the prayer box on Day 27.
Have you done it yet???
If you have—great! Now think of someone else you can show kindness to. _____
If you haven't, try your very best to do it today. **Ask God to help you.**

The story so far...

- David had wanted to show kindness to Hanun.
- But Hanun sent David's men back with their beards half shaved off and their bottoms showing!
- Hanun had insulted God's people, and insulted God. That meant war...

The Ammonites hired lots of extra soldiers (Arameans, also called Syrians) to help them fight.

The Israelite army was led by Joab and his brother Abishai.

READ
2 Samuel 10v9-14

Joab divided his army in two to fight the Ammonites and Arameans.

What did the **Arameans** (Syrians) do? (v13)
a) they fought
b) they fled

What did the **Ammonites** do? (v14)
a) they fought
b) they fled

Wow! The Arameans and Ammonites ran away! Then David won a battle against the Arameans, and loads of kings became David's servants. (v15-19)

 THINK SPOT

Before the battle, Joab didn't know if he'd win or not. But see what he said...

_____ _____ _____ _____ _____

_____ _____ _____ (v12)

_____ _____ _____ _____ _____

PRAY Things may not work out for us. And God may answer our prayers differently from how we expect. But **God always does what's right for His people!** Thank Him for this, and trust Him!

We'll come back to the story of King David on Day 50.

DAY 31 LET'S JOIN JOHN

Today we start reading **John's Gospel**. It's a book that a guy called John wrote. And it's all about **Jesus**! (Gospel means 'the good news about Jesus'.)

*Put a tick next to the facts you think are **true** about John.*

A John was one of Jesus' closest friends (called **disciples**). ☐

B He was the disciple Jesus hated. ☐

C John was known as '**the disciple Jesus loved**'. ☐

D John was a famous basketball player. ☐

E His brother was James the disciple. ☐

F John's parents were Zebedee and Salome. ☐

G His parents were Zebra and Salami. ☐

H John also wrote the Bible books *Revelation, 1 John, 2 John and 3 John.* ☐

ANSWERS: *Facts A, C, E, F and H are all true.*

John spent a lot of time with Jesus. So he was a great person to write a book about Jesus. We can learn loads about Jesus by reading John's book!

Turn to the next page.

xtb — John 20v31

So why did John write his book about Jesus?

READ
John 20v31

Use the **flag code** to find out the first reason.

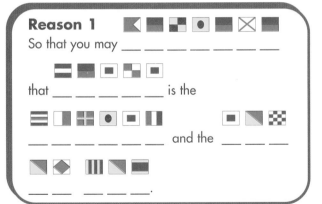

Reason 1

So that you may ＿ ＿ ＿ ＿ ＿ ＿

that ＿ ＿ ＿ ＿ ＿ is the

＿ ＿ ＿ ＿ ＿ ＿ ＿ and the ＿ ＿ ＿

＿ ＿ ＿ ＿ ＿ ＿ .

In his book, John tells us about many of the miracles that Jesus did. And he tells us many of the amazing things Jesus said. John tells us all these things to help us know that Jesus is the **Christ** or **Messiah**.

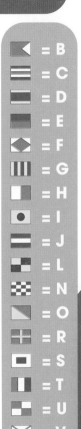

= B
= C
= D
= E
= F
= G
= H
= I
= J
= L
= N
= O
= R
= S
= T
= U
= V

Christ and **Messiah** both mean the same thing: *the King who God promised would rescue His people*. John wrote his book to show us that **Jesus** is the King who can rescue us!

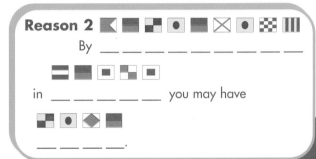

Reason 2

By ＿ ＿ ＿ ＿ ＿ ＿ ＿ ＿ ＿

＿ ＿ ＿ ＿ ＿ ＿

in ＿ ＿ ＿ ＿ ＿ ＿ you may have

＿ ＿ ＿ ＿ ＿ .

John uses the word **LIFE** 36 times in his book! He wants us to know that if we trust Jesus to **rescue** us from sin, we can **live** with Him for ever in heaven!

PRAY

Ask God to help you understand John's book, as we read it. Ask Him to help you BELIEVE that Jesus is the Christ and God's Son.

DAY 32 THE WORD ON THE STREET

 John 1v1-4

READ
John 1v1-2

Who or what does John talk about in those verses?

The W_____

Who does John mean when he talks about **the Word**? *Use yesterday's **flag code** to find out.*

He's talking about **JESUS**! Now read verses 1 and 2 out loud. This time, replace 'the Word' by saying 'Jesus' instead.

We're already learning some amazing facts about Jesus...

FACT 1:
JESUS IS GOD (v1)
John's whole book is all about this amazing fact!

FACT 2:
JESUS HAS ALWAYS BEEN AROUND (v2)

What else can we learn about Jesus?

READ
John 1v3-4

FACT 3:
JESUS CREATED THE WORLD, THE UNIVERSE, EVERYTHING! (v3)

FACT 4:
JESUS BRINGS LIFE AND LIGHT TO THE WORLD (v4)
John mentions **LIFE** and **LIGHT** loads in his book. He wants us to understand that trusting Jesus is the only way to **LIFE** with God in heaven. *We'll read more about Jesus being our **LIGHT** tomorrow.*

PRAY

Read the facts again. Is anyone more amazing than Jesus??? And <u>you</u> can know <u>Him</u>! Get excited and thank God!

DAY 33 LIGHT AND WRONG

 John 1v5-9

John is telling us all about Jesus. He says that Jesus is the '**LIGHT** of men'.

What does light help us to do?

- **see things clearly** ☐
- **light up paths for us** ☐
- **stop us bumping into things!** ☐

Jesus is like a **LIGHT** to people. He shows us the truth about ourselves. He helps us to see the sin in our lives. And He shows us the way to God!

READ
John 1v5

Sadly, many people won't have anything to do with Jesus. They are like people living in complete **DARKNESS**. They need Jesus (the light) to help them see how they should live.

READ
John 1v6-9

Who else did God send into the world (v6)?

- *Ron* ☐
- *John* ☐
- *Joan* ☐

Did you know?

This isn't the same John whose book we're reading. This is **John the Baptist**. God sent him to tell people about Jesus, so they'd be ready for Him.

John the Baptist wanted everyone to know that they needed Jesus to turn their lives around. So that they could start living for God and not for themselves.

Do you know anyone who doesn't want Jesus in their life?

_____

_____

(Maybe you can tell them about Jesus, like John the Baptist did!)

PRAY

You can pray for those people right now! Ask God to turn their lives around, so that they grow to love Jesus.

John has told us loads of amazing facts about Jesus! Here are two of them...

1. JESUS MADE THE WORLD! *(John 1v3)*

2. JESUS IS GOD'S <u>LIGHT</u> FOR THE WORLD *(John 1v9).* **He shows up the wrong things we do. And He shows us the way to God!**

So what do you think people did when Jesus came into the world?

a) welcomed Him

b) held a huge party for Him!

c) refused to welcome Him

READ
John 1v10-11 to find out

UNBELIEVABLE! People **refused to believe** that Jesus was God, who had created the world. They refused to believe that Jesus was their Rescuer. Many of them hated Him. Even many of God's special people (called Jews). But it's not **all** bad news...

READ
John 1v12-13

What is the great news for anyone who **does** believe that Jesus came to rescue them? *(The answer is written backwards.)*

NERDLIHCS'DOGEMOCEBYEHT

THEY _____

_____

_____

HOW COOL IS THAT???

Everyone who trusts Jesus to rescue them from sins becomes one of **<u>GOD'S CHILDREN</u>**! If you're a Christian, God is your **Father**. He looks after you, cares for you and **loves** you!

Do you want to know how to become one of God's children? Then turn to page 15 of your 'Who will be King?' booklet.

PRAY

Thank Jesus that He has made it possible for you to become one of God's children!

DAY 35 JESUS IS GOD!

Neesa is starting a new school soon, and she wants to know what the teachers are like. So she asks her friend, Abby, because Abby is taught by them and knows them.

READ
John 1v14-18

John the Baptist knew all about Jesus, so he can tell us a lot about Jesus.

Wow! They were hard verses to understand! But verse 14 sums them up for us. Read verse 14 again. Then use the words below to fill in the missing words. (*All of the answers are in verse 14*).

GLORY   LIVED   FLESH
TRUTH   GRACE   WORD

1 The W_____ became F_____ (human) and L_____ among us.
The Word means Jesus! He came down from heaven to live on earth as a human. Even though He's God!

2 The people saw Jesus' GL_____.
They saw the amazing miracles He did. Things only **God** could do.

3 Jesus was full of GR_____ and T_____.
GRACE means that Jesus has given people far more than they **deserve**. Everyone has disobeyed God and **deserves** to be punished.

But Jesus became a human and died on the cross to take the punishment in our place. So that anyone who trusts Jesus can become one of ***God's children***! That's far more than anyone deserves!

PRAY   Jesus is God! He loves us so much that He lived on earth as a human, and even died for us! Spend time thanking Jesus for His **grace**!

DAY 36 # IT'S ALL ABOUT JESUS!

God had promised to send someone to rescue His people, the Jews. This person was called the **Christ** or **Messiah**. Many people wondered if John the Baptist was this Rescuer...

READ
John 1v19-23

Was John the **Rescuer** (Christ, Messiah) that God had promised? (v20)
Circle the right answer. **YES / NO**

Was he the prophet **Elijah**? (v21)
YES / NO

Was he the **Prophet** mentioned in Deuteronomy? (v21) **YES / NO**

Was John the **voice** that Isaiah had talked about? (v23) **YES / NO**

> *Did you know?*
>
> 700 years earlier, a man called Isaiah had said that someone would come to tell people to get ready for Jesus the Rescuer. That person was *John the Baptist*!

READ
John 1v24-28

> What gives **you** the right to baptise people?

We'll find out more about John's kind of baptism in two days' time. But John had something more important to say...

> It's not about me! There's someone here who is far more important than me!

John was talking about **Jesus**. John didn't want to be the centre of attention. He wanted everyone to know about **Jesus**, not himself.

Do **you** seek attention and popularity? Or do you want **Jesus** to get the attention instead, so that people are talking about Him?

THINK SPOT

PRAY Ask God to help you be less self-centred. Ask Him to help you tell people about Jesus, like John did.

DAY 37 THE LAMB OF GOD

 If you could be any **animal**, what would it be?

 **READ** John 1v29

Use the **shape code** to see which animal John the Baptist said Jesus was like.

— — — — — — — — —

In Bible times, a lamb was killed and offered to God as a **sacrifice**. If someone had sinned against God, they would say sorry to Him and then offer Him a gift, such as a lamb.

John called Jesus the **Lamb of God** because Jesus would be killed as a sacrifice to God. But why did Jesus have to die?

READ John 1v29

SHAPE CODE

A = ■
B = ■
D = ■
E = ●
F = ●
G = ●
H = ●
I = ◆
K = ◆
L = ◆
M = ◆
N = ★
O = ★
R = ★
S = ✚
T = ✚
U = ◣
W = ◣
Y = ◣

✚ ★ ✚ ■ ◆ ● ■ ■ ◣ ✚ ● ●
— — — — — — — — — — —

✚ ◆ ★ ★ ● ✚ ● ● ◣ ★ ★ ◆ ■
— — — — — — — — — — — — — —

When Jesus died on the cross, He took the punishment <u>we</u> deserve for all our sin. If we trust Him to, Jesus takes away all the sins we've ever done! So we can be friends with God!

 THINK SPOT

Has Jesus taken away <u>your</u> sins? Do you want Him to?

PRAY

Think about wrong things you've done. Now thank God that Jesus can take those sins away and you can forget about them.

DAY 38 THAT'S THE SPIRIT!

John the Baptist is telling everyone about Jesus.

> *Jesus is far greater than me. He is God's Son!*

READ
John 1v30-31

Unscramble the **backwards** words to see the special thing John did.

John B_____
D E S I T P A B

people with W_____
R E T A W

That means he dunked people in the river!

Did you know?

People got baptised by John to show they wanted to be forgiven and cleaned from sin. Water couldn't clean them. But **Jesus** could! By dying, like a lamb, to take their punishment. And by giving the Holy Spirit to help them live for God.

READ
John 1v32-34

Jesus didn't need to be baptised because He never sinned. His baptism was **different...**

---

xtb John 1v30-34

What amazing thing happened to Jesus?

The H_____
Y L O H

S_____ came down
T I R I P S

to Jesus like a D_____
E V O D

God gave His Spirit to Jesus to show that Jesus really was His Son. The amazing truth is that Jesus gives the Holy Spirit to **everyone** who becomes a Christian! The Holy Spirit helps Christians to live for God!

PRAY

Thank God for giving the Holy Spirit to all Christians. Ask God to help you live more for Him and less for yourself.

Daniel thinks Arsenal are great. He watches them on TV all the time.

Christians should get even more excited about **Jesus** than Daniel does about football!

READ
John 1v35-39

These 2 guys were **disciples** of John the Baptist. That means they **learned** from Him about God. What did they do when John told them that Jesus was the lamb of God? **Tick** two answers.

they followed Jesus ☐

they laughed at Him ☐

they called Jesus 'teacher' and wanted to learn from Him ☐

THINK SPOT

Are YOU excited about Jesus? Do you want to learn from Him? Then you should read the Bible more and more!

<u>Here's an idea:</u>

Find an older Christian (a parent or Sunday School teacher). Ask them to read the Bible with you once a week. You could begin with John's Gospel!

READ
John 1v40-42

When Andrew realised that Jesus was God's Rescuer, what was the **first thing** he did? (v41)

ran around clucking like a chicken ☐

told his brother about Arsenal ☐

told his brother about Jesus ☐

Daniel is so excited about Arsenal, he **tells his friends** all about them.

Christians are excited about **Jesus**! They want to tell all their friends and family about Him! Who will **you** tell about Jesus this week? _____

_____

PRAY

Dear God, help me to get excited about Jesus. Please give me the courage to tell my friends and family all about Him.

DAY 40 FOLLOW THE LEADER

John 1v43-50

Yesterday we saw Andrew and Peter become Jesus' first _disciples_. That means they will follow Jesus and learn from Him.

READ
John 1v43-46

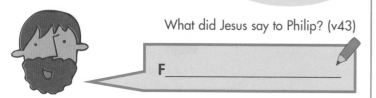

What did Jesus say to Philip? (v43)

> F_____

Philip realised that Jesus was the great **Rescuer** that the Old Testament says so much about. Who did Philip tell about Jesus? (v45)

> N_____

• Jesus wants _us_ to follow Him and live for Him.

• He wants us to understand that He can rescue us.

• And He wants us to tell other people about Him.

READ
John 1v47-50

Now fill in the gaps in the conversation between Jesus and Nathanael.

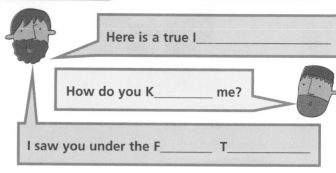

> Here is a true I_____

> How do you K_____ me?

> I saw you under the F_____ T_____

Jesus knew all about Nathanael, even things that seemed impossible to know! And He knows all about **you** too! What you look like, what you do, what you think.

What did Nathanael work out?

> You are the S_____ of G_____

PRAY

Father God, thank you for sending your Son Jesus to rescue me. Thank you that He knows all about me. Please help me to follow Jesus and become more like Him.

DAY 41 STAIRWAY TO HEAVEN

Andrew, Peter, Philip and Nathanael believe that Jesus is **God's Son**. They've decided to follow Him and learn from Him. Jesus told them that they would see amazing things...

 John 1v51

READ
John 1v51

What would the disciples see? *Take the first letter of each picture to find out.*

You will see _ _ _ _ _ _ _ open,

and _ _ _ _ _ _ _ travelling up and down

on the _ _ _ _ _ _ _

The **Son of Man** is <u>Jesus</u>. How could angels use Jesus like a staircase???

Did you know?

The book of Genesis tells us about a dream that Jacob had. In it he saw a huge stairway going from heaven to earth. Angels were travelling up and down it. The stairway **linked** Jacob to God. God promised always to be with Jacob. (Genesis 28 v12-15)

What's that got to do with Jesus?

When Jesus died and came back to life, He became the **link** between God and humans. Like a staircase leading up to heaven. By trusting in Jesus, we can get to know God! Jesus is the only way to God and life with Him in heaven.

Do you want to know more? For the free booklet **Why did Jesus come**? write to: XTB, 37 Elm Road, New Malden, Surrey, KT3 3HB. Or email: alison@thegoodbook.co.uk

PRAY

Thank God that He wants you to know Him, and one day, live with Him. Thank Him for sending Jesus to make that possible.

DAY 42 — WINE SIGN

In Chapter One we've discovered some amazing things about **Jesus**...

- He's **God's Rescuer** (Christ/Messiah)
- He's the **Son of God**
- He's the **only way** to know God and one day live with Him in heaven.

But the disciples <u>don't</u> know all this yet. They need some signs to help them. *Take the first letter of each pic to see what kind of signs Jesus was going to give them.*

_ _ _ _ _ _ _ _

Did you know?

Miracles are like **signposts**. They point to <u>who</u> Jesus is, so that we can believe in Him and live with Him for ever in heaven. (John 20v30-31)

Read about Jesus' <u>first</u> miracle.

READ
John 2v1-11

What did Jesus do?

a) Jesus filled empty jars with water.
b) Jesus turned wine into water.
c) Jesus turned water into wine.

Who believed in Jesus after seeing this miracle? (v11)

a) His mother.
b) His disciples.
c) The bride.

This was Jesus' first miracle. It pointed to <u>who</u> He really is. It showed His **glory** (how great Jesus is).

The disciples **didn't** understand everything about Jesus. Do <u>you</u>?

THINK + PRAY

The disciples **did** believe in Jesus. Do <u>you</u>?

Talk to God about your answers. Ask Him to help you <u>understand</u> and <u>believe</u> what you read about Jesus in the Bible.

DAY 43 TEMPLE TROUBLE

 John 2v12-17

What time is it?
Draw it on the clock face.

Crack the code to see what time it was in today's story.

_ _ _ _ _ _ _ _ **TIME**

It was **Passover** time—a time to remember how God rescued His people when they were slaves in Egypt.

So we'd expect God's temple to be full of <u>excited</u> people, getting ready to celebrate Passover. But use the code again to see what time it was in the temple...

_ _ _ _ _ _ **TIME**

The temple was full of <u>greedy</u> people, using it like a market place! Imagine church full of stalls and sellers, sheep and shoppers! Let's find out what Jesus thought about that...

READ
John 2v12-17

Clock Code

 = A

 = E

 = K

 = M

 = O

 = P

 = R

 = S

 = T

 = V

What did Jesus call the temple? (v16)

my F_____'s house

Jesus is God's <u>Son</u>. He was rightly angry that His Father's temple was being used as a market place.

Draw what Jesus did. (v15)

Read Psalm 69v9. This psalm was written by King David. But it's also about <u>Jesus</u>! It says that Jesus is devoted to His Father's house (the temple). When the disciples saw what Jesus did in the temple, they remembered David's psalm. (*That's what v17 means.*)

PRAY
Sometimes it's right to be angry about things we know are wrong. *E.g. if you see someone being bullied in your class.* If you see something like that, ask God to help you to act in the way He wants you to, even when that's difficult or could make you unpopular.

Imagine if someone came into your school classroom and started throwing the desks about! How would you and your teacher feel?

Draw your faces.

You

Your teacher

Jesus had been tipping over tables in the temple. Let's see what the Jewish leaders thought about that...

READ
John 2v18-25

Use these words to fill in the gaps.

temple   prove   miracle   three

What **m**_____ can you show us to **p**_____ you have the right to do this?

Destroy this **t**_____, and I will raise it again in **t**_____ days.

Jesus was standing in the Jewish temple when He said this. But what 'temple' was He really speaking about? (v21)

His b_____

Did you know?

Jesus was talking about <u>Himself</u>. He was going to die a painful death. But three days later God would bring Him back to life! This showed that Jesus was God's Son. He had the <u>right</u> to clear out the temple.

Lots of people saw Jesus' miracles, and believed in Him. But their faith wasn't going to last. Many of Jesus' followers gave up on Him later on. (*This is in John 6v66.*)

Jesus knew this. He knows <u>exactly</u> what everyone is like. (v25)

THINK + PRAY

It's great that you're reading the Bible to get to know Jesus better. But sadly, some people <u>give up</u> on following Jesus later. If you really want to follow Jesus, ask Him to help you never to give up.

DAY 45 BORN AGAIN

Pat O'Malley
Bill O'Hara } *Which of these three met Jesus?*
Nick O'Demus

OK, OK, it's a trick question! But now you know how to say the name of the man who meets Jesus in today's story. He was called **Nicodemus**...

READ
John 3v1-8

Now try the XTB True–False Quiz

Nicodemus was a Pharisee, one of the Jewish leaders. (v1)
True / False

Nicodemus knew that Jesus had come from God. (v2)
True / False

You can go back inside your Mum to be born again. (v4)
True / False

Nicodemus was right—you <u>can't</u> go back inside your Mum's tum! What did Jesus tell him? (v5)

> N_____ can enter the Kingdom of God unless he is born of
> w_____ and the S_____

In the Old Testament, God promises to sprinkle clean water on His people to clean them from their wrongs, and to give them His Spirit. (Ezekiel 36v25-27)

Nicodemus was a teacher of the Old T, so he should have known this.

Read verse 8 again. We can't see the **wind**. But we <u>can</u> see what it does on a windy day! And though we can't see the **Holy Spirit**, we <u>can</u> see the huge effect the Spirit has on people's lives.

THINK + PRAY

Everyone needs to be **born again**. We need to be washed clean from our wrongs, and to start again with God's Spirit helping us to live for God. If you're a follower of Jesus, then you've been 'born again'. Thank God for His Spirit. Ask Him to help you to live for Him every day. If you're not a follower of Jesus yet, or you're not sure, ask God to help you learn more about this in the next few days.

DAY 46 LIFTED UP

Jesus has told Nicodemus that he needs to be born again. But there's more that Nicodemus needs to know...

Jesus is an

_ _ _ - _ _ _ _ _ _ _ _

READ
John 3v9-13

What name did Jesus give Himself? (v13)

The S_____ of M_____

This title is used in the Old T about the Christ (Messiah). Jesus often used this title when talking about Himself.

Where had Jesus come from? (v13)

H_____

Jesus came from heaven, so He was the **best** person to teach Nicodemus (and us!) about heavenly things (v11). Jesus was an **eye-witness**.

Jesus will be

_ _ _ _ _ _ _ _ _ _

READ
John 3v14-15

What did Moses lift up? (v14)

In the Old T, Moses made a bronze snake. God said that anyone who looked at it would be cured from deadly snakebites. (Numbers 21v8-9)

Who else would be lifted up? (v14)

Jesus was going to be 'lifted up' too—when He was dying on the cross. And anyone who trusts in Jesus, won't just be saved from a snakebite! What will they have? (v15)

E_____ life

PRAY

Wow! The only way to live with God for ever in heaven is by believing in Jesus. Tomorrow we'll see exactly how Jesus made that possible. For now, thank God for His Son Jesus, who came from heaven to save us.

DAY 47 THE MOST FAMOUS VERSE

 John 3v16

We've been listening in on Jesus' conversation with Nicodemus. *Use the Arrow Code to see what Jesus has said so far...*

We need to be _ _ _ _ _ _ _ _ _ _

Jesus came from _ _ _ _ _ _

Jesus will be _ _ _ _ _ _ _ _ _ _ _

Now Jesus is going to tell Nicodemus the most famous verse in the Bible. (But Nicodemus doesn't know that!)

READ
John 3v16

Arrow Code

⇧ = A
⬈ = B
⬂ = D
⬇ = E
⬉ = F
⇦ = G
⬊ = H
⬆ = I
⬋ = L
⬋ = N
⬅ = O
⬉ = P
◁ = R
◁ = T
▽ = U
▷ = V

For God **I**_____ the world so much that He gave His only **S**_____, so that everyone who **b**_____ in Him may not die but have **e**_____ life.

Who sent Jesus into the world? ⟨_____⟩

Why did God send Jesus?
because He
l_____ us

God's everlasting love for us is the reason He sent Jesus. To find out more read ***God's Rescue Plan*** on the next page.

PRAY Father God, thank you that You love me so much that You sent Jesus to rescue me. Amen

Why not try to learn today's verse from memory?

GOD'S RESCUE PLAN

Why did God rescue us—and **who** is the Rescuer? *John 3v16* explains it.

This is the reason for the Rescue Plan. God's **everlasting love** for you and me. He wants us to know Him and to be His friends. But there's a problem. SIN gets in the way.

What is Sin?

We all like to be in charge of our own lives. We do what **we** want instead of what **God** wants. This is called Sin.

Sin gets in the way between us and God. It stops us from knowing Him and stops us from being His friends. The final result of sin is death. You can see why we need to be rescued!

...that He gave His only Son...

God sent Jesus to be our Rescuer—to save us from the problem of sin.

How did Jesus rescue us?

At the first Easter, when Jesus was about 33 years old, He was crucified. He was nailed to a cross and left to die.

As He died, all the sins of the world (all the wrongs people do) were put onto Jesus. He took all of our sin onto Himself, taking the punishment we deserve. He died in our place, as our Rescuer, so that we can be forgiven.

Did you know?

Jesus died on the cross as our Rescuer—but He didn't stay dead! After three days God brought Him back to life! Jesus is still alive today, ruling as our King.

...so that everyone who believes in Him may not die but have eternal life. (*John 3v16*)

When Jesus died He dealt with the problem of sin. That means that there nothing to separate us from God any more. That's great news for you and me!

We can know God today as our Friend and King—and one day live in heaven with Him for ever.

Have YOU been rescued by Jesus? Turn to the next page to find out more...

AM I A CHRISTIAN?

Not sure if you're a Christian? Then check it out below...

Christians are people who have been rescued by Jesus and follow Him as their King.

> **You can't become a Christian by trying to be good.**

That's great news, since you can't be totally good all the time!

It's about accepting what Jesus did on the cross to rescue you. To do that, you will need to **ABCD**.

A **Admit** your sin—that you do, say and think wrong things. Tell God you are sorry. Ask Him to forgive you, and to help you to change. There will be some wrong things you have to stop doing.

B **Believe** that Jesus died for you, to take the punishment for your sin; that He came back to life, and that He is still alive today.

C **Consider** the cost of living like God's friend from now on, with Him in charge. It won't be easy. Ask God to help you do this.

D **Do** something about it! In the past you've gone your own way rather than God's way. Will you hand control of your life over to Him from now on? If you're ready to ABCD, then talk to God now. The prayer will help you.

A prayer

Dear God,
I have done and said and thought things that are wrong. I am really sorry. Please forgive me. Thank you for sending Jesus to die for me. From now on, please help me to live as one of Your friends, with You in charge.   **Amen**

> **Do you remember Jesus' promise?**—"everyone who believes in Him shall not die but have eternal life." *John 3v16*

> **Jesus welcomes everyone who comes to Him. If you have put your trust in Him, He has rescued you from your sins and will help you to live for Him. That's brilliant!**

DAY 48 **TWO WAYS TO LIVE**

Spot six differences in the pics.

On Day 33 we saw that Jesus is like a **LIGHT** to people. He shows us the truth about ourselves. He helps us to see the sin in our lives. But some people don't want to be in the light...

READ
John 3v17-21

Fill in the gaps from v19.

'people love the **d**_____
rather than the **l**_____ because
their deeds are **e**_____.'

People run away from the light (away from Jesus) because they want to **keep on** sinning. They prefer to do what <u>they</u> want instead of what <u>God</u> wants.

Jesus told Nicodemus that people like that are already condemned (judged). They are found **Guilty** and must be punished. (v18)

Write GUILTY under the picture.

BUT we don't have to run <u>away</u> from God's light. We can run <u>towards</u> it instead, and have our sins forgiven.
Fill in the gaps from v18.

'whoever **b**_____
in Jesus is not condemned, but
whoever does **n**_____ believe
stands condemned already.'

If we <u>believe</u> in Jesus, and come to Him to be forgiven, then we are found **Not Guilty** and won't be punished.

Write NOT GUILTY under the picture.

THINK + PRAY

Ask God to show you the wrong things you have done this week. Tell Him you are sorry and ask Him to help you to change. Thank Him for sending Jesus so that you can be forgiven.

DAY 49 A TALE OF THREE PEOPLE

 **xtb** John 3v22-30

Person One = **John A** (the Disciple)

John A <u>wrote</u> about Jesus.

*Cross out the **X**'s to see something John wrote about Jesus.*

• 'Jesus performed this **XFXIXRSXTX** miracle in Cana in Galilee; there He revealed His **XGXLXOXRXYX** and His disciples **XBEXLXIEXVXEXDX** in Him.' (John 2v11)

Person Two = **John B** (the Baptist)

John B <u>spoke</u> about Jesus.

*Cross out the **Y**'s to see what he's said so far.*

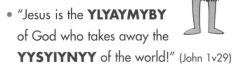

• "Jesus is the **YLYAYMYBY** of God who takes away the **YYSYIYNYY** of the world!" (John 1v29)

• "I tell you that He is the **YSYOYNY** of **YGYOYDY**." (John 1v34)

John B has been busy <u>baptising</u> people (dunking them under water as a sign that they want to be forgiven and washed clean from sin).

But now Jesus has turned up, and <u>He</u> is baptising people too. Will John get jealous...?

READ John 3v22-30

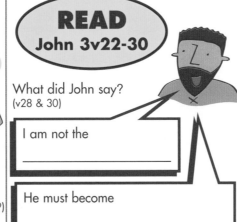

What did John say? (v28 & 30)

> I am not the _____

> He must become _____

> I must become _____

John says Jesus is like a bridegroom—the most important man at a wedding (v29). John is the bridegroom's friend who helps the bridegroom. John isn't jealous at all. In fact he's <u>happy</u> to serve Jesus, God's Son!

↙ Write <u>your</u> name here.

Person Three = _____

John A <u>wrote</u> about Jesus. John B <u>spoke</u> about Jesus. ***What about you?*** Think of someone you could tell about Jesus this week. How will you do it?

e.g. send a letter/email, show them an XTB page, invite them to church...

PRAY Ask God to help you do what you've planned.

DAY 50 THE ONE FROM ABOVE

John 3v31-36

We've reached the end of chapter three of John's book. These last verses are all about **Jesus**—but they don't use His name! They start by calling Him 'the one who comes from above'...

READ
John 3v31-36

These verses are a bit tricky. Here's the XTB Xplanation:

- Jesus comes from heaven. He is **greater** than all. (v31)

- He tells us what He has **seen** and heard, but people don't believe Him. (v32)

- He is full of God's Spirit, and speaks God's **words**. (v34)

- God loves His Son, **Jesus**, and has put everything in His power. (v35)

- Whoever believes in Jesus has eternal life, but whoever **rejects** Jesus will never share in that life. (v36)

*Fit the **blue words** into the puzzle. The **yellow boxes** will spell out another word.*

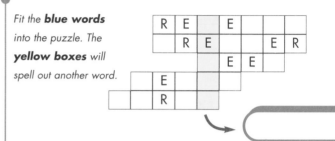

Believing in **Jesus** is the <u>only</u> way to be right with God and one day live with Him in heaven.

Do you remember looking at v36 when we were going through the **'Who will be King?'** booklet? Turn back to **Day 9** to see what we learnt then.

THINK+PRAY

Verse 36 is about a <u>choice</u>. Have you made that choice yet?
- If you already believe in Jesus, and are following Him as King of your life, then thank Jesus for this. Ask Him to help you keep on living for Him every day.
- If you're not sure if you believe in Jesus (or if you want to) ask an older Christian to talk to you about it. And ask God to help you understand and believe what they tell you.

*Use the **Flag Code** to uncover the story so far...*

FLAG CODE

A =  J = S =

B = K = T =

C = L = U =

D = M = V =

E = N = W =

F = O = X =

G = P = Y =

H = Q = Z =

I = R =

The book of **2 Samue**l starts with the deaths of

_ _ _ _ and his son

_ _ _ _ _ _ _ _

David became the new

_ _ _ _
just as God had promised.

David captured

_ _ _ _ _ _ _ _
and made it his royal city.

David brought the Ark of the Covenant to Jerusalem. It reminded the Israelites that

_ _ _ _ _ _ _

_ _ _ _ _ _ _

Find out more on the next page.

David was God's chosen king, ruling over God's people. Let's flick back to chapter 8 to see what kind of king he was.

READ
2 Samuel 8v15

Rewrite verse 15 in your own words, to describe what kind of king David was.

David was a good king. But he wasn't perfect! There's only <u>one</u> perfect King in the world:

_ _ _ _ _   _ _ _ _ _

THINK + PRAY

As we have read 1 & 2 Samuel, David has been a good example for us to follow. We've seen how he **trusts God**. (eg: when fighting against Goliath.) We've seen him show huge **kindness** to an enemy. (eg: when he was kind to Jonathan's son Mephibosheth.) And today we've been reminded that he was **just and fair**, doing what was <u>right</u> for his people. Think carefully about your own life. Are <u>you</u> like David? Do you want to be? Think hard, and then talk to God about your answers.

DAY 52 **HOME ALONE**

Yum... those look great!

And smell even better!

I'll take one. Nobody will know...

DON'T TOUCH!

DON'T TOUCH!

When Tom saw the cakes he knew they weren't for him. But he went to have a closer look anyway. The smell was so good that his mouth started watering. So he took one!

Today's story about King David is a bit like Tom and the stolen cake. It's a sad tale...

READ
2 Samuel 11v1-4

What time of year was it? (v1)

> When kings go to
> **w**_____

But King David <u>didn't</u> go.
Who did he send instead? (v1)

> **J**_____

While Joab was leading the army, David was hanging around in his palace. One evening, while walking on the flat roof of the palace, he saw a beautiful woman.

What was her name? (v3)   **B**_____

Bathsheba was married. But that didn't stop David! He saw her and he wanted her. So he had her brought to the palace, where he slept with her.

Did you know?

One of God's laws says that you mustn't take someone else's wife or husband (Exodus 20v14). David was <u>disobeying</u> God.

More about David tomorrow...

THINK + PRAY

When David saw Bathsheba he should have stopped looking straight away. Instead, he chose to find out more about her. Then he gave in to temptation and took her. When <u>you</u> are tempted to do something wrong, walk away from it! Ask God to help you.

The Bible promises that God will always help us when tempted. This promise is in 1 Corinthians 10v13.

2 Samuel 11v5-13

David had disobeyed God. He had taken another man's wife. Maybe he thought no-one would know what he'd done. But then he got a message from Bathsheba...

READ
2 Samuel 11v5

What was her message? (v5)

I am **p**_____

Bathsheba was going to have a baby. But her husband Uriah was away with the army, so everyone would know that <u>he</u> couldn't be the father. So David came up with a sneaky plan. He'd bring Uriah back to give a report. Then Uriah would go home, sleep with his wife, and think <u>he'd</u> got her pregnant.

But the plan didn't work...

READ
2 Samuel 11v6-13

Did Uriah go home to his wife? (v9)   **Yes / No**

Use these words to fill in the gaps.

camped   not   Joab   wife   ark

The **a**_____ and the men of Israel and Judah are staying in tents, and **J**_____ and his officers are **c**_____ in the open fields.

How could I go home to eat and drink and sleep with my **w**_____? I will **n**_____ do such a thing!

Uriah believed it would be <u>wrong</u> to relax at home while the rest of the army were at war. So he refused to do it!

David's rotten plan had failed. Tomorrow we'll see what he plans next...

THINK + PRAY

On Day 51 we saw that David is often a good example for us to follow. But not this time!!! Are you ever tempted to cover things up when you've done something wrong? Ask God to help you to be honest, and to own up when you're in the wrong.

DAY 54   A HORRIBLE PLAN

xtb   2 Samuel 11v14-27

David's rotten plan (to make Uriah think that he'd got Bathsheba pregnant) hadn't worked. But that didn't stop David! Now he planned something even worse...

READ
2 Samuel 11v14-17

David wanted to have Uriah <u>killed</u> in battle. Did his plan work? (v17)

Yes / No

David's horrid plan worked. Uriah was killed in battle.

Now David could make Bathsheba his wife...

READ
2 Samuel 11v26-27

Bathsheba became David's wife, and later gave birth to a son. It looked like David had got away with it.

BUT how does verse 27 <u>end</u>?

> **But...**
>
>

God knew <u>everything</u> that David had done. And He was **not** pleased! *Tomorrow we'll find out what God does about it...*

PRAY

<u>Nothing</u> we do is hidden from God! He knows everything about us. He knows all the good things we do and say and think. And He knows all the bad things too. How does that make you feel? Talk to God about it now.

DAY 55 FOUND OUT!

David is a liar and a murderer. Will God do nothing about it? No! He sends Nathan to see David, with a story to tell...

"There were two men, one rich and the other poor."

"The rich man had loads of sheep and cows."

"The poor man had just one little lamb."

"The poor man loved his lamb like one of his own children."

"But then a traveller came to visit the rich man."

"The rich man could have killed one of his own sheep to feed his guest."

"But instead he killed and ate the poor man's lamb!"

This was a clever story, as David was about to find out...

READ
2 Samuel 12v1-7a
This means the first part of v7.

How did David feel when he heard the story? (v5)

a) Puzzled
b) Pleased
c) Angry

David was <u>furious</u> with the rich man, and said he deserved to **die**. But what did Nathan tell David? (v7a)

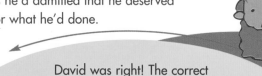
You _____

David had been found out! He was just like the rich man in the story. And by his own lips he'd admitted that he deserved to die for what he'd done.

THINK + PRAY

David was right! The correct punishment for sin is death. That's why Jesus had to **die**, to take the punishment <u>we</u> deserve. More about this tomorrow, but for now, spend some time thanking Jesus for taking that punishment in your place.

Read yesterday's picture story again.

Like the rich man in that story, David took what wasn't his (Uriah's wife). Let's see what God said about that...

READ
2 Samuel 12v7-12

In verses 7 and 8 God reminds David of all the great things He has done for David. How many times does God say 'I' in these verses?

Wow! God had given David **so much**! He had no need to take another man's wife (and life).

God would rightly punish David for disobeying Him (v9-12). Later on in 2 Samuel we'll read about that coming true.

READ
2 Samuel 12v13-14

What did David say? (v13)

> I have

David was right. He <u>had</u> sinned. The right punishment for his sin was death. But what did Nathan tell him? (v13)

> The LORD

David <u>deserved</u> to die for what he had done. But God **forgave** David, and **rescued** him from the death penalty.

Does that sound familiar? The Bible tells us that we <u>all</u> sin, and that the right punishment for sin is death. BUT, if we admit our sin (as David did), and put our trust in Jesus, then God will **forgive** us and **rescue** us from the punishment we deserve. (*This promise is in 1 John 1v9.*)

THINK + PRAY

Grace is God's HUGE kindness to people who don't deserve it. God showed His <u>grace</u> to David by forgiving him. How has God shown His grace to <u>you</u>? Think hard, then thank God for His amazing grace.

xtb 2 Samuel 12v15-23

Imagine you disobey your mum by playing football inside. You break her best vase! You say sorry. She <u>forgives</u> you.

Do you have to leave your family? Can you talk to your mum as normal?

<u>But</u> there are consequences (bad results). Perhaps your football is taken away or you have to pay for a new vase.

God <u>forgave</u> David, so David could still know and talk to Him. But there were *consequences* (results) of his sin. God said that David's newborn baby would die...

READ
2 Samuel 12v15-17

When the baby became ill, what did David do? (v16-18)

He **p**_____ to God, he didn't **e**_____ and he **l**_____ on the ground.

David was forgiven, so he could still talk to God—about how upset he felt about his baby.

READ
2 Samuel 12v18-23

How did David react to his baby's death? (v20)

a) He went home and wept.
b) He went to God's temple and worshipped.
c) He went outside for a walk.

Strange! While the baby was alive, David kept pleading with God. But now that the baby was dead, David <u>accepted</u> God's answer to His prayers. He didn't turn against God. David **trusted God** to carry out His perfect plans.

THINK SPOT

Why did God let David's baby die? To show that sin matters and brings bad results. Do you ever think that because God will forgive you, sin doesn't matter? Sin <u>does</u> matter!

THINK + PRAY

God always answers our prayers. But sometimes the answer is 'No'. We may not understand why, but we can be sure that God is doing the right thing. Do you find that hard? Talk to God about it now.

DAY 58 A SON IS BORN

READ
2 Samuel 12v24–25

What was David's new son called? (v24)

S_____

God also gave him <u>another</u> name—**Jedidiah**.
Crack the code to see what that means.

_ _ _ _ _ _   _ _ _ _ _ _   _ _ _ _ _

God <u>loved</u> Solomon. He would become the next king after David. He was the one who would build a temple for God.

Did you know?

God took David's <u>sin</u> (in taking Bathsheba from Uriah) and used it for His own <u>good</u> purposes (the birth of Solomon). How cool is that!

Flick back to the beginning of chapter 11. What time of year was it? (11v1)

When kings go to w_____

All through the story of David and Bathsheba, the Israelites have been at war with the Ammonites. But now Joab, the leader of the Israelite army, is about to win it...

READ
2 Samuel 12v26-31

Did David capture the enemy city of Rabbah? (v29)   **Yes / No**

David's victory was a sign that God had forgiven him. It was <u>God</u> who gave him victory.

PRAY

Sometimes life is a mess. But God can bring good out of <u>any</u> situation, however awful. Thank Him for this, and ask Him to help you trust Him when things are tough.

DAY 59 **EVERLASTING LOVE**

Psalm 51v1-2

 THINK SPOT

What do you do when you've messed up? Do you brave it out, pretending you've done nothing wrong? Or hide in your room, feeling terrible? Or wish you could go back in time to change what you did?

David had messed up—big time! But he didn't cower in his room. He admitted his sin to God. And he wrote a psalm about it. (A psalm is a prayer or song to God.) *We're going to read that psalm in the next few days.*

READ
Psalm 51v1-2

Did you know?

sin • faults • transgressions • iniquity • evil
David uses all these words to write about his *sin*. Sin is doing what <u>we</u> want instead of what <u>God</u> wants.

David knew he had sinned. But he also knew what <u>God</u> is like. How does David describe God's **love**? (v1)

God's everlasting love never runs out; never fails; never gives up. And because of God's fantastic <u>love</u>, David knows he can ask God for <u>mercy</u>.

Did you know?

Mercy is when God does <u>not</u> give us what we deserve. David deserved to be punished for his sin. But instead he asked his merciful God to forgive him.

What does David ask God to do with his sin? (v2)
W_____ it away.

If you look in a mirror and see mud on your face, you can wash it off. But you <u>can't</u> wash away the sin inside you! You can't clean up your own sin. But **God** can! He can wipe it away completely.

PRAY Read verses 1 and 2 aloud as your own prayer to God. Thank Him for His everlasting love. And thank Him for sending Jesus so that your sin can be washed away.

Psalm 51v3-9

READ
Psalm 51v3-9

Hmm... there's some tricky stuff there! Let's pick out the main bits...

1 David had sinned against Uriah by taking his wife and then murdering him. But <u>who</u> does David say he has sinned against? (v4)

All sin is against **God**. He is our loving Creator. But when we sin we are ignoring His good rules for our lives.

2 How long has David been sinful? (v5)

a) Since taking Bathsheba.
b) Since he was a child.
c) Since he started to grow inside his mother.

Did you know?

Do you have a baby brother or sister? Even if they seem perfect now, they'll soon start proving how sinful they are! Sin isn't just doing wrong things. Sin is about what we're like <u>inside</u>, in our hearts. We all want to run our lives our own way, instead of letting God be our King.

3 Verse 6 says God wants to see
t_____ in our lives.

God <u>sees</u> everything. And He wants **truth** to run right through us. David had been <u>lying</u> to others and to God. He had hidden what he had done with Bathsheba—but God brought it out into the open.

1—David had sinned against <u>God</u>.
2—He was sinful before he was <u>born</u>.
3—He had <u>lied</u> to God.

Did this mean everything was <u>hopeless</u> for David? *Copy the **red letters** (in order) to find out.*

_ _ _ _ _ _ _   _ _ _ _

What a great way to describe being forgiven! All David's sin had been washed away (v7). He was **clean**.

PRAY

Imagine a l-o-n-g list of all your sin. Now imagine God washing it all away, leaving it whiter than snow. That's what it's like to be forgiven. How does that make you feel? Talk to God about it now.

DAY 61 HEART DISEASE

Can you feel your pulse? Try putting two fingers lightly on your wrist, or the side of your neck.

The beat of your pulse shows that your heart is doing it's job and working well. But some people have **heart disease**. Their heart doesn't work well, and they tire easily.

Yesterday we saw that everyone is born with heart disease! Not physical heart disease, but spiritual heart disease. We are all born **sinful** (Psalm 51v5).

Now read what David asks of God...

READ
Psalm 51v10-12

What does David ask? (v10)

Create in me a **p**_____
h_____, O God.

I'm not a heart surgeon! If my physical heart goes wrong, I need an expert to give me heart surgery. The same is true for my spiritual heart. **I** can't clean it from sin. **I** can't fill it with God's Holy Spirit. But **God** can!

Find these words in the wordsearch. Some are written backwards!

HEART
DISEASE
SIN
SPIRIT
PURE

```
O N L     N I S
T I R I P S Y G
D I S E A S E O
T R A E H D
P U R E
```

What do the leftover letters spell (in order)? _ _ _ _ _   _ _ _

Only **God** can give us pure hearts, to love and serve Him wholeheartedly.

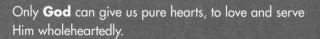 **PRAY** Read verses 10–12 again, aloud, as your own prayer to God.

DAY 62 TIME TO TELL

Spot six differences between Grace and Sally.

"I've sinned against God but He forgave me."

"I've never let God down."

If you were feeling terrible about letting God down, which of these girls would you want to talk to—Grace or Sally?

King David knew exactly what it was like to be sinful, so he was a great person to tell other sinners about God...

READ
Psalm 51v13-19

Fill in the gaps.

I will teach sinners your ways, and they will **t**_____ **b**_____ to you. (v13)

O Lord, open my lips and my mouth will declare your **p**_____. (v15)

praise
back
turn

Did you know?

The Old Testament listed how and when to make **sacrifices** (gifts) to God. But David knew that God first looks at the **heart**—to see if people hate sin and love God. The only way to make a right sacrifice (v16-19) was by having a heart that's right with God.

David longed to use his voice for God:
—to tell sinners how to **turn back** to God and be forgiven
—to **praise** God and tell others how wonderful He is.

THINK + PRAY

Think about your voice. How can you use it for God today?

_____
_____
_____

Use your voice now to thank God that He's so wonderful, and ask Him to help you tell others about Him too.

By the way—Sally may think she's never let God down, but she's wrong! Everyone sins.

DAY 63 THE GENERATION GAME

We're going to finish this issue of XTB with another of David's psalms. This time he's falling over himself to tell us how wonderful God is!

Did you know?

exalt • praise • extol • proclaim
You'll meet some of these words in David's psalm. They all mean telling others (and God!) how great God is.

READ
Psalm 145v1-7

What does David call God? (v1)

My G_____ and K_____

David is a king—but he knows that **God** is the real King!

How l-o-n-g is David going to praise God for? (v2)

a) 27 minutes
b) 8 years
c) Always

How G-R-E-A-T is God? (v3)

a) He's a little bit great, but not as great as David Beckham.
b) He's very great, but not as great as the President of the United States
c) His greatness is so HUGE it can't be measured (fathomed)!

*Use the **Face Code** to see what else David said in his psalm.*

A E G I N O R T

One _ _ _ _ _ _ _ _ _ _ _ _ will tell another. (v4)

This means that adults will tell children, grannies will tell grandchildren, uncles will tell nephews and so on...

THINK + PRAY

Think of someone from another generation who tells <u>you</u> about God. *Write their name here.*

Thank God for this person. Ask Him to help them know the best way to tell you how totally GREAT God is.

David is bursting to tell us how good God is...

READ
Psalm 145v8-16

Different versions of the Bible use slightly different words in verses 8 and 9. (Circle) the ones that are in _your_ Bible.

gracious   compassionate   loving   patient   merciful   good   tender   slow to anger   kind

God is so **loving** that He is **merciful** (He doesn't treat us as we deserve). Instead He is **gracious** (showing huge kindness to us even though we don't deserve it).
No wonder David wants to praise Him!

Take the first letter of each pic.

_ _ _ _ _   _ _ _ _ _ _ _

Which verse says God always keeps His promises?   **v____**

Do you have a favourite promise from the Bible? Write in and tell me _what_ Bible verse it is, and _why_ it's your favourite. I'll send you a free XTB Promise Pencil. It has Psalm 145v13 written on it: 'The Lord is faithful to all His promises'.
Write to: XTB, The Good Book Company, 37 Elm Road, New Malden, Surrey, KT3 3HB **or email:** alison@thegoodbook.co.uk

There are some very important truths in today's verses:
• God is loving
• God is merciful
• God is good
• God always keeps His promises

<u>Underline</u> one that you particularly want to remember today.

Why did you choose that one?

PRAY   Thank God for being so wonderful. Ask Him to help you get to know Him even better as you keep reading His book, the Bible.

DAY 65 NEAR OR FAR?

God is the real King. He's so powerful, there's nothing He can't do!

It doesn't sound like God will have time to bother with me. I'm nobody...

Do <u>you</u> ever feel like Sam? If so, the last part of Psalm 145 is just what you need to hear...

READ
Psalm 145v17-21

What does David say God is like? (v17)

> The Lord is **r**_____
>
>   in all His ways.

Did you know?

When God is called **righteous** it means that He is always in the right, and does what is right. God never thinks, does or says anything wrong!

What else does David say? (v18)

> The Lord is **n**_____ to all
>
>   who call on Him.

Wow! Our amazing, powerful God —who always does right—is **near** to us! He wants us to call on Him. He wants us to talk to Him (about every part of our lives, not just the BIG stuff). How cool is that!

Jot down some stuff you can talk to God about. Add things from your own life, your family, friends, school, and the world.

PRAY Our wonderful God will <u>always</u> listen to your prayers. He is **near** to you. Talk to Him now about some of the things on your list.

TIME FOR MORE?

Have you read all 65 days of XTB? Well done if you have!

How often do you use XTB?
- Every day?
- Nearly every day?
- Two or three times a week?
- Now and then?

You can use XTB at any time...

In the morning.

At bedtime.

When you get back from school.

When do <u>you</u> read XTB?

XTB comes out every three months. If you've been using it every day, or nearly every day, that's great! You may still have a few weeks to wait before you get the next issue of XTB. But don't worry!—that's what the extra readings are for...

EXTRA READINGS
The next four pages contain extra Bible readings from the book of 1 Samuel. If you read one each day, they will take you 26 days. Or you may want to read two or three each day. Or just pick a few to try. Whichever suits you best. There's a cracking wordsearch to solve too...

Drop us a line...
Why not write in and tell us what you think of XTB:
—What do you like best?
—Was there something you didn't understand?
—And any ideas for how we can make it better!

Write to: XTB, The Good Book Company, 37 Elm Road, New Malden, Surrey, KT3 3HB
or e-mail me:
alison@thegoodbook.co.uk

The extra readings start on the next page

BEFORE DAVID WAS KING...

In this issue of XTB we have learnt about King David from the book of 2 Samuel. These 26 extra readings are like a <u>flashback</u>—to David's earlier life, before he was king...

David and Saul

King Saul quickly became jealous of David, and kept trying to kill him. But David knew that God had promised to make him king, so he <u>trusted</u> God to save him. And God did!

The ideas in the box will help you as you read the verses.

PRAY Ask God to help you to understand what you read.

READ Read the Bible verses, and fill in the missing word in the puzzle.

THINK Think about what you have just read. Try to work out one main thing the writer is saying.

PRAY Thank God for what you have learnt about Him.

There are 26 Bible readings on the next three pages. Part of each reading has been printed for you—but with a word missing. Fill in the missing words as you read the verses. Then see if you can find them all in the wordsearch below. Some are written backwards—or diagonally!

If you get stuck, check the answers at the end of Reading 2

S	P	I	R	I	T	U	J	O	N	A	T	H	A	N
O	H	A	S	E	E	N	E	T	W	L	V	X	T	B
K	I	N	G	D	O	M	S	F	A	M	I	L	Y	D
B	L	U	E	R	A	E	P	S	N	A	C	K	G	E
W	I	N	D	O	W	H	I	S	T	A	T	I	O	N
E	S	C	L	U	C	K	N	A	L	P	O	S	A	I
L	T	W	O	H	U	N	D	R	E	D	R	I	T	M
L	I	A	R	O	T	H	U	R	R	Y	Y	D	S	R
E	N	A	D	A	V	I	D	O	E	S	H	E	L	E
M	E	A	F	R	A	I	D	W	B	I	B	L	E	T
A	S	R	E	H	T	A	F	S	O	F	A	B	L	E
N	J	E	A	L	O	U	S	X	R	W	O	R	L	D

☐ **Read 1 Samuel 17v45**

Flashback 1: *Goliath challenged the Israelite army to fight him—but they were all too scared! But David knew that God was on his side...*

'You come against me with sword and spear and javelin, but I come against you in the **n** _ _ _ of the Lord Almighty.' (v45)

2 ☐ **Read 1 Samuel 17v46-49**

Flashback 2: *David knew that God would give him victory over Goliath. He was right!*

'The whole **W** _ _ _ _ will know that there is a God in Israel.' (v46)

3 ☐ **Read 1 Samuel 18v1-4**

David was now living at King's Saul's palace. He became good friends with Saul's son, Jonathan.

'**J** _ _ _ _ _ _ _ _ made a covenant (binding agreement) with David because he loved him as himself.' (v3)

4 ☐ **Read 1 Samuel 18v5-9**

Everything David did was a success. But that made Saul jealous of David!

'From that time on Saul kept a **J** _ _ _ _ _ _ eye on David.' (v9)

5 ☐ **Read 1 Samuel 18v10-11**

Ever since Saul had turned away from God, he had been bothered by an evil spirit. David's harp playing helped Saul, but one day Saul attacked David!

'Saul threw the spear, saying to himself, "I'll pin David to the **W** _ _ _ ." But David dodged him twice.' (v11)

6 ☐ **Read 1 Samuel 18v12-16**

Everything David did was a success, because God was with him.

'In everything he did he had great success because the **L** _ . _ _ was with him.' (v14)

7 ☐ **Read 1 Samuel 18v17-19**

Saul told David he could marry Saul's daughter, Merab, as long as David fought in battles. Saul hoped David would die fighting the Philistines!

'Saul said to himself, "I will not raise a hand against David. Let the **P** _ _ _ _ _ _ _ _ _ _ do that!"' (v17)

8 ☐ **Read 1 Samuel 18v20-25**

Saul offered his second daughter, Michal, to David for the price of 100 Philistine foreskins (skin at the end of the penis). Saul hoped those Philistines would kill David!

'Saul's **p** _ _ _ was to have David killed by the Philistines.' (v25)

9 ☐ **Read 1 Samuel 18v26-30**

David killed twice as many Philistines as needed, without being hurt! Saul's wicked plan had failed!

'David and his men went out and killed **t** _ _ **h** _ _ _ _ _ _ _ Philistines.' (v27)

10 ☐ **Read 1 Samuel 19v1-3**

Saul told Jonathan that he wanted to kill David. But Jonathan warned David about his father's plans.
'Jonathan warned David,
"My **f** _ _ _ _ _ is looking for a chance to kill you."' (v2)

11 ☐ **Read 1 Samuel 19v4-7**

Jonathan reminded Saul that David had risked his own life to save the Israelites from Goliath. So Saul promised not to kill David.
"The Lord won a great
v _ _ _ _ _ _ for Israel. When you saw it, you were glad." (v5)

12 ☐ **Read 1 Samuel 19v8-12**

Although he'd promised not to, Saul again tried to kill David with his spear. Then Saul sent men to David's house to kill him. 'Michal let David down from a
w _ _ _ _ _ _'
and he ran away
and escaped.' (v12)

13 ☐ **Read 1 Samuel 19v13-17**

Michal helped David escape. Then she put a statue (idol) into David's bed, and pretended it was David!
'Michal took an idol and laid it on the bed, covering it with a garment and putting some **g** _ _ _ ' _ hair at the head.' (v13)

14 ☐ **Read 1 Samuel 19v18-24**

David escaped and joined Samuel. Every time Saul's men came near David, they started prophesying (singing praise to God). When Saul himself went to catch David, he started to prophesy too!
'But the **S** _ _ _ _ _ of God even came upon Saul, and he walked along prophesying all the way to Naioth.' (v23)

15 ☐ **Read 1 Samuel 20v1-4**

Jonathan agreed to do anything David wanted, to save him from Saul.
'Jonathan said to David, "Whatever you **w** _ _ _ me to do, I'll do for you."' (v4)

16 ☐ **Read 1 Samuel 20v5-13**

David and Jonathan made a plan. David wouldn't come to the feast at Saul's table. Jonathan would then te David if Saul was angry or not.
'David said, "If Saul says, 'All right,' will be safe; but if he becomes angry, you will know that he is
d _ _ _ _ _ _ _ _ _
to harm me."' (v7)

17 ☐ **Read 1 Samuel 20v14-1**

Jonathan asked David to show kindness to his family. David kept th promise years later. (2 Samuel 9)
'Jonathan said, "Do not ever cut off your kindness from my
f _ _ _ _ _."' (v15)

18 ☐ **Read 1 Samuel 20v18-2**

Jonathan said that he would use arrows as a secret sign to tell David about Saul's plans.
"I will shoot three **a** _ _ _ _ _ a it, as though it were a target." (v20)

9 ☐ **Read 1 Samuel 20v24-33**

When Saul saw that David hadn't come to the feast, he was furious. He even tried to kill his son Jonathan! Saul threw his **S** _ _ _ _ at Jonathan to kill him, and Jonathan realised that his father was really determined to kill David.' (v33)

0 ☐ **Read 1 Samuel 20v34-42**

Jonathan used some arrows to warn David about Saul, as they'd agreed. Jonathan shouted to the boy with him, but the message was really for David. Jonathan shouted, "**H** _ _ _ _ _! Go quickly! Don't stop!"' (v38)

1 ☐ **Read 1 Samuel 23v14-18**

We're skipping ahead a few chapters to see how Jonathan helps David again. This time Jonathan reminds David to trust in God's promise that David will be the next king. 'Jonathan said, "Don't be **a** _ _ _ _ _ _. My father Saul won't be able to harm you. You will be king over Israel."' (v17)

22 ☐ **Read 1 Samuel 23v19-23**

Some people from a town called Ziph agreed to help Saul catch David. 'Saul said, "Find out for certain where David is, and who has **S** _ _ _ him there."' (v22)

23 ☐ **Read 1 Samuel 23v24-29**

Saul was chasing David round a hill, when a messenger arrived to tell Saul he had to come back and fight the Philistines. God had saved David! 'Saul and his men were on one **S** _ _ _ of the hill, and David and his men were on the other side, hurrying to get away from Saul.' (v26)

24 ☐ **Read 1 Samuel 24v1-7**

Saul went into a cave to go to the toilet. It was the cave David and his men were hiding in! David crept up and cut Saul's robe. 'David crept up unnoticed and cut off a corner of Saul's **r** _ _ _.' (v4)

25 ☐ **Read 1 Samuel 24v8-15**

David showed Saul the cut off corner from his robe—as proof that David wasn't trying to kill Saul. 'David shouted, "Look at the piece of your robe I am holding. I could have killed you, but instead I only **C** _ _ this off."' (v11)

26 ☐ **Read 1 Samuel 24v16-22**

Saul says David will be king of Israel one day. As we know from the book of 2 Samuel, Saul is right! 'Saul said, "I know that you will surely be king, and that the **k** _ _ _ _ _ _ of Israel will continue under your rule."' (v20)

WHAT NEXT?

XTB comes out every three months. Each issue contains 65 full XTB pages, plus 26 days of extra readings. By the time you've used them all, the next issue of XTB will be available.

ISSUE TEN OF XTB
Issue Ten of XTB explores the books of John and 1 and 2 Kings.
- The Gospel of **John** tells us all about Jesus. Read about some more of the miracles that pointed to <u>who</u> Jesus is.
- Find out more about David's son Solomon, and the kings who came after him, in the books of **1 and 2 Kings**.

Available December 2004 from your local Christian bookshop—or call us on **0845 225 0880** to order a copy.

Look out for these three seasonal editions of XTB:
Christmas Unpacked, Easter Unscrambled and *Summer Signposts*. Available now.

XTB Joke Page

All sent in by *Dan Levett*.

What do ants take when they are ill?
Antibiotics!

What dog smells of onions?
A hot dog.

What lies on the ground, 100 feet up in the air, and smells?
A dead centipede.

What do you call a skeleton in your cupboard?
The Hide and Seek World Champion.

Is your free book missing?
This issue of XTB should include a free copy of the booklet 'Who will be King?'. If yours is missing write to us at the address below or phone 0845 225 0880 and we will send you a copy.

Do <u>you</u> know any good jokes?
—send them in and they might appear in XTB!

Do you have any questions?
...about anything you've read in XTB.
—send them in and we'll do our best to answer them.

Write to: XTB, The Good Book Company, 37 Elm Road, New Mald Surrey, KT3 3HB **or e-mail me:** alison@thegoodbook.co.uk